JBIOG
Marsh
Herda, D. J.

**Thurgood Marshall : civil rights
champion**

Justices of the Supreme Court

THURGOOD MARSHALL

Civil Rights Champion

D. J. Herda

ENSLOW PUBLISHERS, INC.

44 Fadem Road
Box 699
Springfield, N.J. 07081
U.S.A.

P.O. Box 38
Aldershot
Hants GU12 6BP
U.K.

Library of Congress Cataloging-in-Publication Data

Herda, D. J., 1948–
    Thurgood Marshall: civil rights champion / D. J. Herda.
        p.   cm.— (Justices of the Supreme Court)
    Includes bibliographical references and index.
    ISBN 0-89490-557-0
    1. Marshall, Thurgood, 1908-1993—Juvenile literature. 2. Judges—
United States— Biography—Juvenile literature. 3. United States. Supreme Court—
Biography—Juvenile literature. 4. Civil rights workers—United States—Biography—
Juvenile literature.
    [1. Marshall, Thurgood, 1908-1993. 2. Judges. 3. United States. Supreme Court—
Biography. 4. Afro–Americans—Biography.]
    I. Title. II. Series.
    KF8745.M34H466   1995
    347.73'2634—dc20
    [B]
    [347.3073534]
    [B]   94-31224
                                                                        CIP
                                                                        AC

Printed in the United States of America

10 9 8 7 6 5 4 3 2 1

⚖ CONTENTS ⚖

Speaking Out

In the spring of 1925, a young African-American man from Baltimore, Maryland, was hired to work as a dining-car porter for the B&O railroad. He put on his uniform for the very first time and discovered that his pants were considerably shorter than his long, lanky legs. The young man told his supervisor about the problem. The solution, of course, was simple: Get a longer pair of pants.

But the supervisor, a career railroad worker with many years of seniority, didn't see things quite that way. Perhaps he viewed the young boy as just another African-American teenager who was too big for his britches. Perhaps he simply didn't have time to worry about the boy's problem. In any event, the supervisor gave the young man a choice: Either wear the pants or get off the train.

Thurgood Marshall decided he would wear the pants.[1] It

was an injustice he would remember the rest of his life—the type of thing he would make a career out of battling the remainder of his years on earth. He would spend twenty-six of these years as a Justice of the Supreme Court of the United States.

Appointed by President Lyndon Johnson in 1967, Marshall spent approximately a quarter century on the nation's highest court. While there, he became one of America's foremost crusaders for social justice, the only Supreme Court Justice ever to defend an accused murderer.

After Marshall gained entrance to the Maryland state bar in 1933, he entered private practice and served as legal counsel for the Baltimore branch of the National Association for the Advancement of Colored People (NAACP). He specialized in civil rights cases, which in those days earned a lawyer respect, but little money. Eventually, according to longtime friend James Poling, Marshall "built the largest law practice in Baltimore and still couldn't pay his rent."[2]

But all that had changed by the time Marshall received his nomination to the Supreme Court. He was a respected member of the legal community and a shrewd defender of civil rights. Marshall quickly earned a reputation as a no-nonsense Justice who had no sympathy for anyone who trampled on the rights of African Americans—or anyone's rights, for that matter.

But his aggressive defense of civil rights earned him nearly as many enemies as friends. Some of his enemies were in very high places, indeed. That became all too clear to Marshall when he entered the hospital in 1970, suffering from a life-threatening case of pneumonia. President Richard M. Nixon was anxious to see a vacancy on the bench so that he could add a more conservative Supreme Court Justice.

6

Thurgood Marshall was the first African American ever to serve on the United States Supreme Court. Appointed by President Lyndon Johnson (right), Marshall quickly earned a reputation as a no-nonsense Justice.

He asked hospital officials for a health report on the ailing Justice. Marshall authorized the release of his records to the president, but not without first writing in bold letters on the cover of the report, "Not yet!"[3]

Over the years, Marshall suffered several bouts with serious illness: a heart attack, bronchitis, blood clots, hearing loss, and glaucoma. Yet, throughout them all, he insisted that his was a lifetime appointment, and he intended to serve it.

But on June 27, 1991, the feisty defender of civil rights had a change of heart and announced that he was ready to resign. "I'm old," he said of his decision. "I'm falling apart."[4] In interviews, he said that he was ready to take life easy for a while—an action hardly in keeping with his personality.

Yet those closest to him had to admit that Marshall had earned the rest. "He's done more than anyone could possibly expect of him," said attorney Karen Hastie Williams, Marshall's godchild and former law clerk. "He's devoted more than fifty years of his life to public service. I've no doubt this was the most difficult decision of his life."[5]

Marshall's retirement from the Supreme Court left behind a legacy of judicial brilliance that may never be matched. As an aggressive young lawyer, he won twenty-seven of the thirty-four cases he argued before the Supreme Court. Perhaps his greatest triumph came while working as an attorney for the NAACP in the landmark 1954 case, *Brown* v. *Board of Education of Topeka, Kansas*. This case ended once and for all the "separate but equal" policy in the nation's school systems. The plaintiff's case was for the most part designed and carried out by Marshall, whom Roger Wilkins of the NAACP once called "the embodiment of our twentieth-century advances."[6] Marshall's greatest victories, though, came when he was on the Supreme Court bench, where he contributed to decisions such as *New York Times* v. *United States, Roe* v. *Wade, United States* v. *Nixon, University of California Regents* v. *Bakke,* and *Immigration and Naturalization Service* v. *Chadha.*

Thurgood Marshall was a light in a nation engulfed in darkness. But he never forgot his roots. He never failed to recall his humble beginnings.

"Son," his father once told him, "if anyone ever calls you a nigger, you not only got my permission to fight him, you got my *orders* to fight him."[7]

They were words that Marshall would remember his entire life. These words would haunt him in his later years. These words would spur him on to judicial greatness.

9

The Early Years

Born to Norma and William Marshall in 1908, young Thurgood knew what it meant to be poor. His mother was a teacher at an integrated Baltimore primary school. His father was a steward at the all-white Gibson Island Country Club on Chesapeake Bay. His great-grandfather had been brought to Maryland from the African Congo and was a slave for years before finally winning his freedom.

Upon graduating with honors from Douglas High School, Thurgood went on to receive an A.B. degree *cum laude* from Lincoln University in 1930. He enrolled as a law student at Howard University in Washington, D.C., where, he said, ". . . for the first time, I found out my rights."[1]

Thurgood's own mother found him to be lazy and irresponsible, a poor student in school, someone his own uncle once branded a "bum."[2]

Thurgood came to the conclusion early in life that none

of his teachers was likely to fail him when his own mother taught in his school. After all, how would that look? So he rarely participated in classwork, almost never did homework, and—just as he had expected—always passed, even if only by the skin of his teeth.

Not that Thurgood received his grade-school diploma on a silver platter. He worked hard to get it—if not in class, at least after class. In fact, Marshall often credited his superior knowledge of constitutional law to his classroom mischief. Many times he was forced to stay after school and, as punishment for some offense, he would be required to memorize portions of the Constitution.

"Before I left that school," he once said, "I knew the whole thing by heart."[3]

Thurgood also admitted that he had been a spoiled child. He once suffered so badly from a hernia that the doctor who examined him advised his mother to keep him as quiet as possible. He told her to "see that he doesn't do any crying."[4] Thurgood overheard the doctor's advice and, from that moment on, took every advantage of his sickness. He cried when he wanted something from his older brother, cried when he wanted something from his parents, cried when he wanted nearly anything at all.

Finally, Thurgood's mother could take no more. Much to the young boy's surprise, she pulled him aside, wrapped a bandage tightly around his midsection, and "beat the stuffing" out of him.[5]

Thurgood never again resorted to crying to get his way. But he learned a valuable lesson from the experience—something that would serve him well for the rest of his life. He learned to take every possible advantage of a situation, while keeping in mind the nature of the consequences.

As Thurgood grew older, he began to mellow, showing signs that he was beginning to mature into a young man. He worked many jobs during his early years—from delivering hats to working as an errand boy at Hale's Grocery Store in Baltimore. But it was his work on the railroad—alongside his father, who at the time worked for the Baltimore and Ohio—that instilled in him a healthy respect for the work ethic and a desire to achieve. Thurgood saw how hard his father had to work as a porter and, later, as a waiter for the whites-only Gibson Island Country Club on Chesapeake Bay. All this was so that the family could survive in one of the North's most segregated cities. "The only thing different between the South and Baltimore was trolley cars," he once recalled. "They weren't segregated. Everything else was segregated."[6]

Thurgood also learned something from his mother. She worked hard as a schoolteacher yet earned only half as much as white schoolteachers of the day were making. Still, she never complained, just kept on plugging away, one day at a time. She always tried to help the family make ends meet.

"My daddy earned so little that Mama had to work. . . . She was getting a dollar a day. It was awful. Still, to offer a decent life to us, they bought a house, which they couldn't afford. I listened to my parents whisper about their economic desperation, and I finally said, 'Mama, sell the house.'"[7]

His mother insisted that she would do no such thing. She was determined to leave the house to Marshall and his brother. The house was not worth all that much—only about $4,000 at the time. But, it was her way of providing her sons with a better start in life than she had when she was a young child.

Thurgood couldn't bear the thought of his parents struggling from week to week just to get by—and driving themselves to an early grave in the process. Finally, Thurgood called his mother aside.

"Mama," he said, "if you died this morning, we'd sell the [darn] house this afternoon."[8]

The next day the house went up for sale.

His mother wasn't the only source of pride in Thurgood's life. His father, who once worked as a butler for a wealthy white widow, often demonstrated his own strong sense of self-worth. One night, while the widow was sitting in the parlor drinking coffee and brandy with several friends, the woman's pampered pet poodle came in.

"Nanky," she said, "show the people which you would rather be, a nigger or dead."[9] The guests roared with laughter as the dog rolled over on its back with its feet up in the air, as if to say it would rather be dead. Thurgood's father, who had witnessed the incident, took off his butler's coat, grabbed his hat, and walked out the front door. He never went back.

Young Thurgood learned from both of his parents to be proud of his heritage. He learned to defend himself with dignity—and sometimes with his fists—whenever it was required. Most importantly, he learned that no man—white or black—was going to give him anything in life. If he wanted something, if he deserved something, he would just have to figure out a way to get it for himself. That, his parents taught him, was the real secret of life.

As Thurgood grew into manhood, he showed a passion for life that few of his peers matched. Throughout his college years, he worked hard and played hard—sometimes choosing to play at the expense of his studies. Of course, like many men his age, he spent a good many hours of his life pursuing women. Not just any women—but women whom he thought would be ideal candidates for marriage.

One day, Thurgood visited a small Philadelphia Baptist church with several friends. "We went in there," he recalled, "because we learned that's where all the cute [girls] went."[10] Sure enough, there he met an attractive woman named Vivien Burey, a student at the University of Pennsylvania. She had black hair, black eyes, and a vibrant personality.

Thurgood fell in love with Buster—his pet name for Vivien—almost immediately. After only a few dates, he asked her to marry him. When the time finally came for their two families to meet in Baltimore—where the Marshalls lived—everything went along smoothly at first. Then, Marshall's Uncle Fearless walked into the room.

Uncle Fearless pulled Buster aside and said simply that he thought she was a fine young lady. He asked her if she realized that his nephew Thurgood was a bum. Not content with that, he then told Buster's parents the same thing.

Asked once why his own uncle would refer to him as a bum, Marshall admitted that it was because of his reputation as a partygoer and a womanizer. Whether the opinion he had of his nephew was right or wrong, Uncle Fearless went to his grave believing that young Thurgood would never amount to anything.

Still, Buster never for a moment stopped believing in her man. She saw in him someone who was strong, devoted, and dedicated to a cause. She considered marriage to him an honor. So, in 1929, despite promising her parents she would wait to marry until she was out of college, Vivien Burey married Thurgood Marshall, and the two set up house in Baltimore.

Following his graduation the next year, Marshall applied to the law school at the University of Maryland. Within weeks, Marshall received a letter from college president R. A. Pearson, rejecting his application. Maryland, along with most

Despite some family opposition, a young Thurgood Marshall married
Vivien "Buster" Burey in 1929.

other professional schools in the South, rejected African-American applicants—*all* African-American applicants.

Marshall next decided to apply to Howard University Law School in the District of Columbia. Only one thing stood in his way. He could not afford the tuition.

When his mother found out, she insisted her son go forward with his plans. "You're going," she told him. "I'll pawn my engagement and wedding rings to help you."[11] She did just that, never to see them again.

Although he was rejected by Maryland, life at Howard University was good to him. It was there that he met Charles H. Houston, an African-American professor who had distinguished himself at Amherst College and at Harvard Law School. Houston would play a major role in Marshall's life for the next twenty-five years. They would help each other. But, their relationship did have its trying moments.

Marshall said of Houston:

> First off, you thought he was a mean so-and-so. He used to tell us that doctors could bury their mistakes, but lawyers couldn't. And he'd drive home to us that we would be competing not only with white lawyers but really well trained white lawyers . . . . He was so tough we used to call him "Iron Shoes" and "Cement Pants" and a few other names that don't bear repeating. He made it clear to all of us that when we were done, we were expected to go out and do something with our lives.[12]

The stern discipline and never-ending tutoring paid off. In 1933, Marshall graduated first in his class. He opened a small law practice near downtown Baltimore and spent hours thinking about what he could do to change the racist admissions policies of the University of Maryland. Then Marshall got his first break.

Late in 1933, Houston—who had left teaching and moved to New York to set up the National Association for the Advancement of Colored People (NAACP) Legal Defense Fund—convinced the Baltimore branch of the NAACP to hire the struggling young attorney. It didn't take Marshall long to write his former professor, asking, "What is the proposed action on the University of Maryland?"[13]

While Marshall was correct in his assessment of the situation, he was way behind Houston. Houston had months earlier reached the conclusion that the Jim Crow states, states that practiced discrimination against African Americans, would remain segregated until the southern colleges, universities, and professional schools that were supported by African Americans with their tax dollars were forced to put an end to their policies of discrimination.

Marshall learned that Houston and the NAACP were mapping out a careful plan to force integration, the mixing of blacks and whites, upon the South. Marshall was not satisfied. He would not wait for a "master plan" developed by NAACP headquarters in New York. He would confront the University of Maryland by himself.

Since Houston could no longer restrain his former student, he sent Marshall $100 of NAACP money and gave the young attorney a set of simple instructions. "Go, man, go!"[14] Marshall went.

In 1934, Marshall searched high and low for a student he could recommend to Houston as a possible candidate to file a lawsuit against the university. Houston warned Marshall not to open himself up to a charge of barratry (soliciting lawsuits). Finally, Marshall met a young Amherst College graduate named Donald Murray. Murray was intent upon attending law school at the University of Maryland. So, he and Marshall sent a registered letter to the university's president, R. A. Pearson, asking for Murray's admission to the law school. Pearson rejected the application. He said that Murray could more inexpensively attend the all-black Howard University Law School in Washington, D.C.

With his own rejection years earlier in mind, Marshall quickly began preparing documents asking the Baltimore City Court to issue a *writ of mandamus.* This is a court order demanding that something be done. Marshall would try to force the University of Maryland to admit Murray to its law school that September.

It took Judge Eugene O'Dunne only minutes to reach a decision in favor of Murray. He added that no appeal by the university or the state's attorney general could keep Murray out of the classroom on opening day, September 25. Still, the university began planning a strategy to overturn the decision.

When September 25 finally came, the editor of *Afro-American* magazine sent a reporter to the campus to do a feature story on Murray and his historic admittance to the University of Maryland. The reporter later stated that he could not find a single student who welcomed Murray. Everyone the reporter met vowed to get the African-American student out by encouraging teachers to fail him—or by whatever other means possible. But their vows were not fulfilled. Murray graduated in June 1938, the first African American ever to emerge from the university's school of law.

It was perhaps a small victory for Marshall and the NAACP. But it was an important one. For the first time in history, a white court had been forced to admit that the "separate but equal" doctrine practiced for decades throughout the South was not equal. For blacks in America, separate education was anything *but* equal. Now the University of Maryland and other educational institutions throughout the South were forced to realize it, too. The decision was the beginning of an era that would change the face of the nation.

On the Move

Even before Marshall had an opportunity to bask in the glory of his success with the *Murray* case, the University of Maryland was back at it again. Now they were turning away African-American applicants to its schools of law, pharmacy, and journalism. The harder the NAACP fought to open the university to integration, the more resistance it met from school officials.

One day Houston told Marshall about a young man named Roy Wilkins who had been named editor of the NAACP's *Crisis*. He and Marshall were given instructions to wage all-out war on segregation in higher education. The separation by law of blacks and whites had to be stopped—not only at the University of Maryland, but also at other colleges and universities throughout the South. Within days, Marshall began writing a legal brief. He would challenge the denial of black students to enter both Maryland and the University of Texas.

Although he was doing important work now, Marshall was still living a life of near poverty. Then, in 1936, Marshall got the break he had been waiting for. Houston called and asked him to come to New York to be his deputy assistant special counsel for the national NAACP. He told Marshall he would pay him two hundreds dollars a month. Marshall whooped and hollered so loud that Buster ran in to see if he was dying.

Marshall and his wife gathered up their belongings and moved to New York, where they rented a small apartment near the Polo Grounds. Shortly after, Marshall began expanding the work he had begun in Baltimore. He was still trying to stop other southern states from doing what the University of Maryland and the University of Texas had tried to do. Southern colleges and universities were preventing the enrollment of blacks in white institutions by paying their way at northern institutions. This practice had to stop. If only he could find a black student willing to step forward and challenge the segregation laws in court, Marshall was convinced they would win.

On September 27, 1935, a young man named Lloyd L. Gaines wrote to Houston, complaining about his treatment by the Missouri University School of Law. Gaines said that he had applied for admission to the school because of its reasonable rates and emphasis on Missouri law. But instead of granting him admission, university officials pointed out to him Section 9622 of the 1929 Revised Statutes of Missouri. In that section conditions were set out for paying the tuition of Missouri blacks to graduate schools in nearby states. Because Gaines was well qualified for admittance, he could not understand the university's refusal. He wrote to the NAACP for help.

Houston sent Gaines's letter to Marshall, urging him to grab the opportunity the two had been waiting for. Marshall wasted no time. The following January, he finished the brief for *Lloyd L. Gaines* v. *S. W. Canada, Registrar, U. of Missouri*. The brief was filed with Judge Walter S. Dinwiddie in Columbia, Missouri. But Dinwiddie said that there might be trouble at the university if thirty or forty Negroes went there, so he recommended that the action be filed instead in the State Supreme Court in Jefferson City. In that way, according to the judge, the court's finding would affect the entire state. Marshall was convinced that Dinwiddie was afraid to tackle such an emotionally charged issue. According to Marshall, the judge was trying to find a way not to deal with the case. Still, if that's the way it had to be, so be it.

But before Marshall had an opportunity to file the brief in Jefferson City, the University of Missouri board of curators gave Marshall and the NAACP a gift. On March 27, the board passed a resolution saying,

> WHEREAS, Lloyd L. Gaines, colored, has applied for admission to the School of Law of the University of Missouri, and
>
> WHEREAS, the people of Missouri, both in the Constitution and in the Statutes of the State, have provided for the separate education of white students and Negro students, and have thereby in effect forbidden the attendance of a white student at Lincoln University, or a colored student at the University of Missouri, and
>
> WHEREAS, the Legislature of the State of Missouri, in response to the demands of the citizens of Missouri, has established at Jefferson City, Missouri, for Negroes, a modern and efficient school known as

Lincoln University, and has invested the Board of Curators of that institution with full power and authority to establish such departments as may be necessary to offer students of that institution opportunities equal to those offered at the University, and have further provided, pending the full development of Lincoln University, for the payment, out of the public treasury, of the tuition, at universities in adjacent states, of colored students desiring to take any course of study not being taught at Lincoln University, and

WHEREAS, it is the opinion of the Board of Curators that any change in the State system of separate instruction which has been heretofore established, would react to the detriment of both Lincoln University and the University of Missouri,

THEREFORE, BE IT RESOLVED, that the application of said LLOYD L. GAINES be and it hereby is rejected and denied, and that the Registrar and the Committee on Entrance be instructed accordingly.[1]

Until the university had issued that resolution, no educational institution in America had been willing to fight the issue of segregation on a purely racial basis. Instead, they had excluded blacks from white institutions and justified their actions with other, more subtle reasons. Suddenly, Marshall had been handed a blatant declaration that the University of Missouri had based its decision solely on race.

"God, I couldn't believe it when the curators made it clear in their instructions to registrar Canada that Gaines was being rejected solely because of his race. . . . the curators saved the NAACP about a hundred thousand dollars [in legal costs], which it didn't have, by that admission."[2]

It didn't take long for university officials to realize their mistake. Within weeks, three more blacks had applied for admission to the university, and Marshall filed a brief once again with Judge Dinwiddie. The university responded by naming no fewer than six lawyers to defend their position.

Meanwhile, Marshall and the NAACP were beginning to attract national attention. *Time* magazine, *The New York Times*, and the *New York Herald Tribune* all began writing about how the civil rights group was stirring up a revolution in higher education. Houston knew the value of publicity. He pointed out to *Time* reporters that Marshall was already writing briefs demanding an end to segregation in the School of Pharmacy at the University of Tennessee, the medical school of the University of North Carolina, and many other professional schools in Virginia and other southern states.

On July 27, Dinwiddie ruled in favor of the university. *Time* reporters crowded NAACP headquarters with questions about the ruling. The more publicity, the better the NAACP looked in the eyes of the public. Dinwiddie's ruling was only the first round in a long legal battle the NAACP planned to wage, though. It was a battle, they realized, that might go all the way to the Supreme Court of the United States.

The day after the ruling, however, Gaines wrote Houston at the NAACP, saying that he had changed his mind about seeking application to the University of Missouri's law school. Instead he planned to enroll in a master of arts program in economics at the University of Michigan. That in itself wouldn't have been so bad. But Gaines also planned to accept tuition money from the state of Missouri to pay his way at the University of Michigan.

Gaines's announcement threatened to sink the NAACP's case. By agreeing to accept Missouri's long-established policy of paying the tuition of Missouri blacks to northern state universities, Gaines was in effect supporting the policy. At the same time, he was destroying the NAACP's case.

To sidestep the problem, Houston agreed to pay Gaines's tuition at Michigan. The NAACP then continued its pursuit of the case.

But more bad news lay ahead. First, the Missouri Circuit Court refused to order the university to admit Gaines. Then, on December 9, 1937, the Supreme Court of Missouri affirmed Dinwiddie's decisions and that of the circuit court. The battle to admit Gaines to the University of Missouri, it seemed, was lost—at least for the moment. Still, the Supreme Court of the United States remained a last hope. The NAACP prepared to file a motion asking the Court to review the case.

Meanwhile, by 1938, Charles Houston's grueling schedule was wearing him down. He was ready to step down. He nominated Marshall to become the NAACP's chief legal officer in his place, and Marshall accepted. It did not take long for Marshall to achieve his first major victory in the continuing battle against segregation.

On December 12, 1938, the Supreme Court of the United States ruled in favor of Gaines. In writing the Court's opinion, Chief Justice Charles E. Hughes said,

> Here, petitioner's [Gaines's] right was a personal one. It was as an individual that he was entitled to the equal protection of the laws, and the State [of Missouri] was bound to furnish him within its borders facilities for legal education substantially equal to those which the State there afforded for persons of the white race, whether or not other Negroes sought the same opportunity.

In 1938, Thurgood Marshall (left) was nominated to become the NAACP's chief legal officer. He replaced Charles Houston.

It is argued, however, that the provision for tuition outside the State is a temporary one—that it is intended to operate merely pending the establishment of a law department for Negroes at Lincoln University. While in that sense the discrimination may be termed temporary, it may nevertheless continue for an indefinite period by the reason of the discretion given to the curators of Lincoln University and the alternative of arranging for tuition in other States, as permitted by the state law as construed by the state court, so long as the curators find it unnecessary and impracticable to provide facilities for the legal instruction of Negroes within the State. In that view, we cannot regard the discrimination as excused by what is called its temporary character. . . .

The judgment of the Supreme Court of Missouri is reversed and the case is remanded for further proceedings not inconsistent with this opinion.[3]

Following the decision, University of Missouri officials quickly set up a law school for blacks in an effort to maintain the all-white status of the university's law school. Houston and Marshall saw the danger of Gaines enrolling in this school. It would be just one more example of segregation at work. They advised him against it.

After months of legal battles, Houston (now editor of the *Journal of the National Bar Association* in Washington, D.C.) wrote to Marshall about Lloyd Gaines. He said that the last communication between Gaines and Lincoln University library assistant Frank Wethers had been in April. Shortly thereafter, the *St. Louis Post-Dispatch* and the *St. Louis Globe-Democrat* had begun searching for Gaines. All searches were unsuccessful. Houston concluded the letter by suggesting that Marshall put out a request for anyone who knew of Gaines's location to contact the NAACP.

Before long, the national media got hold of the rumors that Gaines had disappeared. Several newspapers and magazines began searching for him, basing searches on tips that he had been seen in Mexico and other places. Some heard rumors that Missouri white racists had paid him to disappear. Others heard that he had been murdered.

Finally, on July 8, 1940, Houston wrote to Neil Dalton, managing editor of the *Louisville* [Kentucky] *Courier Journal.* He pointed out the difficulty the NAACP was having in checking out the rumors of Gaines's whereabouts. Gaines had been seen working in Illinois, spending money in Vera Cruz, and teaching under a false name in Chase City, Virginia, Houston wrote. None of the rumors proved to be true. Finally, on January 1, 1941, the case was dismissed.

Marshall's first United States Supreme Court victory had vanished as quickly as it had appeared—as quickly, in fact, as had Gaines himself. Still, the puzzling affair was not without its rewards. The Gaines case set the legal precedent Marshall and the NAACP would use to eliminate segregation in Oklahoma, Texas, Louisiana, and other states. With *Gaines,* the long-standing practice of providing "separate-but-equal" education for blacks was dealt a crippling blow.

Marshall himself, reflecting upon the curious string of events surrounding *Gaines,* remembered the case as one of his greatest ever. But he never got over having so many people spend so much time and money on Gaines, only to have him disappear into thin air.

Battling for
Civil Rights

A lthough Marshall had gained a considerable amount of
publicity as the attorney behind the victories in the
Gaines and *Murray* cases, his knowledge of constitutional law
was still quite limited. Around this time, he received a telephone call from Tulsa, Oklahoma. The caller was attorney
Amos Hall, a well-known fighter for racial justice. Hall
needed Marshall's help. There was nowhere else to turn.

Hall, as it turned out, had learned of a young black boy,
W. D. Lyons, who had been set up by some whites who had
committed a triple murder. At first Marshall couldn't believe
his ears. What was Hall thinking? Here was Marshall, deeply
involved in defending a Bridgeport, Connecticut black man,
Joseph Spell. Spell had been accused of raping his employer,
Eleanor Strubing. (Marshall said in an interview years later
that he believed Spell was innocent, but proving it in a mostly

white community was not an easy task.) Now Hall was asking him to take on another case. This one involved a black ex-convict who was accused of murdering a white man named Elmer Rogers, chopping up the man's wife after shooting her in the stomach, and then burning down the house with the couple and their four-year-old son inside.

Marshall's first reaction was to tell Hall simply that he had no time. But then he stopped to think. Amos Hall was a self-sacrificing, life-risking African-American man in a state where racial tensions threatened to explode at any moment. He decided to hear the lawyer out. The string of events that Hall had passed along to Marshall would change the course of the NAACP attorney's life.

The information Hall gave intrigued Marshall enough that he decided to do whatever he could to help in the defense of Lyons.

On January 22, Hall called Marshall again to update him. It seemed that a confession had been obtained in the deaths of Elmer Rogers, his wife, and four-year-old son, from a Sawyer Prison Camp convict. Yet, despite that, Lyons remained in custody. Hall then told Marshall that he had heard that a huge bootlegging ring had supposedly been operating out of the office of Oklahoma Governor Leon C. Philips. Hall was convinced that Rogers had been killed because he had a falling-out with the bootleggers and threatened to expose them. After the murders, Hall theorized, someone in the ring must have decided to find an African-American man to take the blame.

Weeks turned into months, and nothing more happened in the case. Lyons remained in custody, but no one had made any attempt to prosecute him. The case took a turn when

Oklahoma attorney Stanley Belden stepped in. He had been hired to represent Lyons, and he learned that Lyons had endured terrible beatings and torture in order to get him to confess that he and another black man named Van Bizzell had murdered the three Rogers' family members. Bizzell, who denied any part in the crime, was released on bond on July 10, 1940, and never brought to trial.

Meanwhile, Belden had spoken to the father, mother, and other relatives of Mrs. Rogers, the murdered woman. Her father insisted that he had enough information about the crime to know that Lyons was innocent. A very suspicious cover-up was going on in the governor's office.

When Marshall got word that Lyons had finally been charged and was due to go to trial in the Choctaw County courthouse on January 27, he boarded a plane for Oklahoma City. The civil rights issues Marshall would confront in Choctaw County would be the same ones he would face the rest of his life. A poor black had been "arrested" by citizens who had no warrant. He had been held for days without being charged or taken before a judge. He had been denied the right to talk to an attorney. He had been beaten and tortured into a "confession" and then forced to confess again only hours later.

In his notes and in telegrams back to NAACP national headquarters, Marshall wrote of the unprofessional atmosphere in the courtroom. The judge puffed on a cigar with his feet high up on the bench. He segregated the court into two parts—whites on one side and blacks on the other. Marshall even told how the white spectators were saying that the "nigger" lawyer from New York [Marshall] hadn't done anything yet.

December 31, 1939. Elmer Rogers, his wife, and their four-year-old son had been murdered in their home near Fort Towson, Oklahoma. The murderer then poured kerosene on their bodies and set fire to the house. Two other sons, eight-year-old James and one-year-old Billie, escaped.

January 2, 1940. Oklahoma governor Leon C. Phillips learned that a Sawyer Prison Camp inmate serving time for having murdered his wife had left the camp, gotten drunk, and was free at the time the Rogers family was shot and axed to death. The convict, who was serving a thirty-year term at the time, was arrested in connection with the murders.

January 5, 1940. Authorities took into custody a twenty-eight-year-old woman who had supposedly "witnessed" the murders.

January 9, 1940. Choctaw County Sheriff Roy Harmon offered a $100 reward to anyone providing information leading to the arrest of the *two* men who had murdered the Rogers family. Harmon provided no explanation as to how he came to believe two men had committed the crime.

January 11, 1940. A twenty-one-year-old man named W. D. Lyons, a black who had served two prison terms—one for chicken stealing and one for burglary—was arrested by a group of white citizens who allegedly had connections to a bootlegging ring, as well as to high political offices. Although Lyons had not been officially charged, he was rumored to be under pressure to confess.

Marshall went on to say that, when he had arrived in town, he had half expected to be attacked by angry whites. By the middle of the trial, however, several white spectators had come up to him and told him what the father of the murdered woman had said. There was something fishy about Lyons's prosecution.

The *Lyons* case turned out to have everything that Marshall had long ago vowed to fight: white criminals framing poor blacks; a lack of lawyers willing to defend poor minorities; police officers and prosecutors holding accused blacks in custody without charging them with a crime; and confessions being beaten out of the poor and helpless. But, with the odds clearly against his client, it was apparent to nearly everyone that there was no way Marshall could win the case in that courtroom.

Sure enough, on January 31, 1941, exactly one year and one month after the murders had been committed, Lyons was found guilty and sentenced to life imprisonment. Although the loss was disappointing, Marshall believed that the Choctaw County jury's decision would eventually be overturned. After all, the Supreme Court of the United States had recently condemned the practice of convicting people on the basis of forced confessions. Lyons's confession had obviously been forced. Medical examiners found the still-fresh bruises on his body just hours before the confession was made.[1]

So on June 4, 1943, the Criminal Court of Appeals of Oklahoma met to begin its consideration of Lyons's request for a rehearing. On August 18, the request was denied. The fifty-page opinion said that the defendant had clearly murdered Elmer Rogers and his wife. In a dissenting opinion,

Judge Thomas H. Doyle said:

> The law is not designed to be a swift engine of oppression and vengeance, but it was and is designed to try and convict men only after due hearing and a fair trial. . . .
>
> I do not believe [Lyons] has been tried and convicted in accordance with law, and he did not have that fair and impartial trial which the law guarantees to one charged with crime. . . . The petition for rehearing should be allowed, the judgment of conviction reversed, and the case remanded to the trial court with direction to grant a new trial.[2]

That same day, the *Lyons* case was appealed to the Supreme Court of the United States, with the help of Marshall, the NAACP, and the American Civil Liberties Union. Everyone was confident, Marshall would later recall, that the Court would reverse the decision and Lyons would be freed. After all, in a March 1943 decision written by Justice Felix Frankfurter, *McNabb* v. *United States,* the Court struck down the convictions of two men. It was found that the men had been arrested, thrown into a barren jail cell for fourteen hours, and subjected to relentless questioning for two days. Frankfurter wrote that a conviction resting on evidence secured through such a flagrant disregard for the laws could not be allowed to stand.

On April 26, 1944, the *Lyons* case was argued before the Supreme Court of the United States. The issue was a landmark one: When a defendant is forced into confessing that he committed a crime, and the first confession is ruled inadmissible, can the state secure a valid second confession only hours later?

On July 5, 1944, the Court responded. Yes, it ruled,

Marshall (left) and members of the NAACP, including Roy Wilkins (right), appealed to the Supreme Court in the *Lyons* case.

Lyons was guilty. Simply stated, the majority of Justices ruled that, although the police beat Lyons into confessing the first time, the effects of the beatings had disappeared by the time he confessed a second time.

Marshall had been defeated. How could this be? It made no sense. If a man was beaten so severely that he confessed to a murder he did not commit, why would he risk receiving still more beatings only a few hours later by changing his confession to not guilty?

The decision was a bitter blow for the NAACP, for Marshall, and for the civil rights movement in general, as well as for Lyons. The defeat left a deep and lasting impression on Marshall. It convinced him that the American legal system was stacked against the poor and minorities. It turned an angry young Baltimore lawyer into a legal machine determined to uphold the Constitution of the United States at any cost.

In an interview some thirty years later, Marshall commented that he still believed Lyons had been innocent. Perhaps, a large number of Oklahomans did also. On May 24, 1965, nearly a quarter century after Lyons had been sentenced to life imprisonment, Oklahoma governor Henry Bellmon pardoned him. Lyons has not been seen or heard from since.

5

The Enemy Within

A fter the bitter *Lyons* defeat, America found itself poised on the brink of World War II in Europe and the Pacific. Many African Americans wanted to help. America, if it found itself embroiled in conflict, would need guns, tanks, planes, and ships. It would need ammunition, canteens, knapsacks, uniforms, Jeeps, tents, and medical supplies.

America's African Americans could help United States industries get ready for war. They could enlist in the military and fight to protect their country. They would do this despite the fact that their country had done little to protect them since the Emancipation Proclamation of 1863.

President Franklin D. Roosevelt, rather than following his own instincts, listened to his advisors and his generals and admirals. They all insisted that African Americans would not serve well in America's military unless they were confined to Jim Crow units. These special units, made up entirely of blacks, were assigned lowly chores such as cooking, cleaning, and handing out supplies to the men—white men—on the front lines.

For the duration of the war, blacks took it. They did their duty as well and as efficiently as any white unit. They distinguished themselves in their country's greatest hour, and they returned home—those of them lucky enough to do so—to resume another battle.

With the end of World War II, Marshall and the NAACP switched gears. They were no longer fighting to protect the rights of black soldiers. Now they were fighting to gain blacks equal access to facilities, to obtain the right to vote, and to gain the right of blacks to enroll in the educational institution of one's choice.

Still fighting for what they believed was their right to segregation, southern universities such as the University of Texas and the University of Oklahoma insisted that the doctrine of "separate but equal" worked and worked well. But "separate but equal" was about to be severely tested.

On January 14, 1946, Ada Sipuel, the daughter of an African-American minister and an excellent student in high school, applied for admission to the University of Oklahoma. University president George Cross personally supported African Americans being admitted to the university. He wrote Marshall and the NAACP a letter stating that Sipuel was being turned down at the request of the board of regents, solely on the basis of her race.

That was all Marshall needed to hear. Now he could file a complaint in the Cleveland County, Oklahoma, court. The complaint was not enough to win his case, though. Marshall and the NAACP did not do any better in the Oklahoma Supreme Court. It too ruled that the university did not have to admit Sipuel.

But Marshall had one more thing on his side. At the same time he was preparing to challenge the university's position in the United States Supreme Court, he was waging another war. He was attempting to have a black man, Heman Marion Sweatt, admitted to the all-white University of Texas. If he could secure a victory there, he knew he would have a fighting chance of convincing the Supreme Court to overturn the Oklahoma Supreme Court decision.

Things did not go as Marshall planned. The *Sweatt* case was bogged down in the Texas court system. In January 1948, the Supreme Court of the United States agreed to hear arguments in the Oklahoma case of Ada Sipuel. The Oklahoma assistant attorney general opened his arguments by insisting that Sipuel could not at the time find facilities anywhere in the state equal to those at the University of Oklahoma. But, he promised that the regents would open a Negro law school promptly if asked to do so.[1]

Justice William O. Douglas, clearly amused by the remark, commented that Ada Sipuel might be an old lady by that time.

Another of the state's attorneys said that Sipuel was not willing to recognize the state's segregation policy. Justice Robert H. Jackson remarked that he was not surprised. She was, after all, African American. The Court went on to rule that Ada Sipuel was entitled to legally secure an education from a state institution. It added that the state had to provide that education for her, just as it did for members of other racial groups.[2]

Marshall and the NAACP had won a clear-cut victory—or so they thought. But the regents of the University of Oklahoma had other ideas. They interpreted the Court's order to provide educational facilities to mean that Oklahoma had to furnish a school of law for Sipuel. They hired three white professors to teach law at the newly founded "Langston University School of Law" and set up classes for Sipuel in room 428 of the state capitol building.

Marshall flew back to Norman, Oklahoma, where another test case was pending. G. W. McLaurin had applied for a program of studies in education at the University of Oklahoma. He had been rejected on the grounds that the state did not accept Negroes in its all-white institutions.

Once again Marshall went to court. This time, he won a judgment from a three-man federal district court panel. It stated that McLaurin was entitled to receive a postgraduate course of study in a state institution.[3] The judgment went on to say that the court had not found Oklahoma segregation laws to be unconstitutional. They were merely inoperative in this particular case.

Once again, university officials sought to sidestep the intent of the court's decision. They allowed McLaurin to register at the university. They insisted, however, that he use a separate toilet. When he went to his first class, he was instructed to sit in what had previously been a broom closet. At the library he was told that he had to read books in a special seciton reserved only for him.

It was a simple and mean-spirited plan to frustrate McLaurin to the point where he would withdraw from the university. But the plan was about to backfire.

At the NAACP's suggestion, nearly fifty black students applied to the university's various schools. The regents were informed that the blacks would have to be admitted to all graduate courses that were not currently provided at the all-black Langston University. To satisfy the legal ruling, the regents quickly opened up ten new courses. Study for blacks would be at separate hours and in separate locations from those for whites.

But such additions to the university's program cost money, so the regents went to the state legislature for additional funding. Suddenly university officials began to see Marshall's strategy unfolding before their very eyes. If the university was going to insist upon providing "separate but equal" educational facilities for blacks and whites, it was going to have to pay a small fortune to do so.

Finally, on June 5, 1950, the Supreme Court of the United States ruled that separate toilets, eating places, classes, classrooms, and housing facilities for blacks at universities were illegal. The Court based its ruling on the Fourteenth Amendment. When a Negro was admitted to the university, he had to receive the same treatment at the hands of the state as students of other races.

A decision by the United States Supreme Court in the case of *Heman Sweatt* v. *University of Texas* came next. The Court declared that Sweatt could not get a reasonable legal education without being admitted to the University of Texas law school. It was one more victory for Marshall and the NAACP. It did, however, fall short of what Marshall had hoped for—a Supreme Court decision that would strike down once and for all the concept of "separate but equal" education.

But there would be time for that later. Now, once again, the nation was faced with a crisis of a different sort—war.

The Korean War broke out on June 25, 1950. Communist and non-Communist forces clashed over the north-south border that had been set up at the end of World War II when Korea had been divided. The 38th parallel separated the Soviet (North Korean) and U.S. (South Korean) zones of occupation. When North Korean forces invaded

South Korea in 1950, the United Nations held an emergency meeting and authorized its members to aid South Korea.

Shortly thereafter, in July 1950, the all-black U.S. Twenty-fourth Infantry Regiment (led mostly by white officers) won the first major victory of the war. They reclaimed the strategic city of Yechon in a bloody sixteen-hour battle. Greatly outnumbered, the unit suffered staggering casualties as it went on to take control of Bloody Ridge, a strategic point on the highway leading into Yechon.

Despite their bravery and a general order from President Harry S. Truman in 1948 that all United States military troops be desegregated at once, blacks in the military continued to receive second-class treatment. Throughout the early months of the war, they were accused and convicted of rape, cowardice in duty, misbehavior, and refusal to follow the orders of a superior officer in numbers far greater than white soldiers were.

The number and severity of complaints filing into the offices of the NAACP steadily increased. Marshall noted that there had been no similar reports of court-martials of white soldiers. He issued a statement saying that the NAACP was ready to defend, with all of its resources, any servicemen who were victims of racial discrimination.[4]

One of the biggest issues here was the way in which the very same blacks who had been labeled as brave heroes one day, often were branded as cowards and traitors the next. It simply did not make sense. The NAACP decided that the only way it would ever get to the bottom of these issues was to send a representative to the Far East to conduct a first-hand investigation. They sent Marshall.

Marshall spent nearly three weeks in Tokyo. He interviewed blacks who were in the stockade with General

This cultural cross section of attorneys of all races would have been an uncommon sight in America during the time of the Korean War.

Douglas A. MacArthur. At the time, MacArthur was in charge of all United States forces in Korea. Marshall found that the white hierarchy in the military was using racism and hatred to weed out the undesirables. Blacks were being discriminated against solely because of their race.

Marshall, though, was still not satisfied that he had gotten all the information he needed. Next, he went to Korea to interview blacks who had been court-martialed, to investigate reports, and to review orders and other records. His findings showed that there were nearly four times as many white soldiers as blacks in Korea. However, nearly two-thirds of the cases taken to trial involved blacks.[5]

The trials were conducted almost exclusively by white judges and commanding officers. They appeared to be rigged against blacks from the start. In one case, Marshall learned of a white officer who openly expressed his hatred of black soldiers. Marshall's investigation turned up many examples of overt, outright racism. It also produced some remarkable statistics. During a period from August through October 1950, thirty-two black servicemen had been convicted of misbehavior in the presence of the enemy. By comparison, just two whites had been convicted of the same crime over the same time period. One of every thirty-two blacks had been sentenced to death. Fifteen of every thirty-two had been sentenced to life in prison. Of these, fourteen received ten, twenty, twenty-five, or fifty years imprisonment. Two of them received sentences of five years. Of the two whites convicted, one received three years, the other five years.[6]

Upon his return to the United States, Marshall made stopovers in several large cities. He shared his findings with the press. Outraged citizens at home—both black and white—demanded to know why such injustices were allowed to happen to blacks in the field. Congress quickly began holding hearings. Orders were passed along to the military: Desegregate or else!

It took several years, but the military finally banned separate facilities and unfair treatment of blacks in the armed forces. Without the work of Marshall and the NAACP, countless blacks in the military might still be suffering the evils of racism.

Even before Marshall had an opportunity to present his full report to the NAACP, the organization had begun representing black servicemen at the United States Army's Review Board. As a result, more than thirty sentences were reduced. Of nine life sentences, six were changed to twenty years in prison. One was changed to fifteen years in prison. One was changed to ten years. Another was completely suspended.

6

The Fall of Segregation

Linda Brown was the seven-year-old daughter of Reverend Oliver Brown. In the fall of 1950, Linda's father took her by the hand and walked her to the Sumner Elementary School in Topeka, Kansas. There, Brown was met by school officials who told him what he already knew. The school board had decided that, although the Browns lived in an integrated neighborhood, Linda could not attend the all-white public school just four blocks from her home. Instead, the girl would have to leave her white and Mexican-American playmates and be bused nearly two miles to a "Negro" school.

Brown went to see Charles Scott. Scott was his friend and former classmate at Topeka High School, and a local attorney for the NAACP. Scott agreed to file suite against the Topeka school board. Marshall saw the moment he had been waiting for. The NAACP and Marshall joined the *Brown* case with four other school segregation cases. All of the cases were presented together under the title *Brown* v. *Board of Education of Topeka, Kansas.*

Marshall then prepared a brief. Working with him were his deputy, Jack Greenberg, some of the best black lawyers in America, and some of the most noted white lawyers working for the ACLU and on law school faculties throughout the country. He then enlisted the aid of nineteen *amicus curiae*, or "friends of the court." They too filed briefs criticizing the treatment of Linda Brown and the concept of "separate but equal" education. Organizations such as the Congress of Industrial Organizations, the American Jewish Congress, the American Civil Liberties Union, the Japanese American Citizens League, the Catholic Interracial Council, the American Federation of Teachers, and the American Veterans Committee, were all firmly against segregation.

Finally, on December 9, 1952, the big day arrived. Marshall and his legal staff prepared to present their oral arguments. This would not be an easy case for Marshall. Sitting across the courtroom from him were nine very serious white men:

- **Chief Justice Fred M. Vinson**, sixty-two years old, a conservative Kentuckian who had been appointed to the Court by Harry S. Truman.

- **Stanley F. Reed**, sixty-eight years old, a Kentuckian who had delivered the crushing decision in the *Lyons* murder case that Marshall had handled years earlier.

- **Felix Frankfurter**, seventy years old, a former Harvard Law School professor and a noted conservative who hated to see anything change unnecessarily.

- **Robert H. Jackson,** sixty years old, the former chief counsel for the United States at the *Nuremburg* trials following World War II.

- **Harold H. Burton,** sixty-four years old, the former mayor of Cleveland, Ohio.

- **Tom C. Clark,** fifty-three years old, the former United States attorney general from Texas.

- **Sherman Minton,** sixty-two years old, a former conservative senator from Indiana.

- **Hugo Black,** sixty-six years old, an Alabaman and former member of the Ku Klux Klan who had somehow managed to put his past behind him and was now considered an outspoken defender of civil liberties.

- **William O. Douglas,** fifty-four years old, a vocal supporter of racial equality.

Of the nine Justices, Marshall was confident of winning over at least two—Black and Douglas. A third, Robert Jackson, was a possibility, but by no means a sure thing. There were two other Justices whose support Marshall would need to win the case. No one—least of all Marshall himself—could predict who might come around to his way of thinking. Marshall prepared to present his opening argument. It focused mainly on the Fourteenth Amendment, which he read aloud:

> All persons born or naturalized in the United States and subject to the jurisdiction thereof are citizens of the United States and of the state in which they reside. No state shall make or enforce any law which shall abridge the privileges or immunities of citizens of the United States; nor shall any state deprive any

person of life, liberty, or property, without due process of law; nor deny to any person within its jurisdiction the equal protection of the laws.[1]

Opposite Marshall in the courtroom were several state's attorneys. They were led by noted constitutional lawyer John W. Davis. Marshall, together with the NAACP, was operating on a very small budget. Davis, a one-time presidential candidate, brought with him all of the money and the social power of the segregated South. In response to Marshall's reading of the Fourteenth Amendment, Davis said:

> The Fourteenth Amendment never was intended to do away with segregation in schools. It is a proper use of the police powers of a state to separate the races if the state believes segregation to be in the interest of common welfare. Segregation in schools is not in conflict with the Constitution as long as equal facilities are provided for the two races. A state has as much right to classify pupils by race as it does to classify them by sex or age.[2]

Then Marshall rose to the challenge presented to him. In a stirring statement, he outlined the reasons the doctrine of "separate but equal" did not work.

> I got the feeling on hearing the discussion yesterday that when you put a white child in a school with a whole lot of colored children, the child would fall apart or something. Everybody knows that is not true. Those same kids in Virginia and South Carolina—and I have seen them do it—they play in the streets together, they play on the farms together, they separate to go to school, they come out of school and play ball together. They have to be separated in school. . . . Why, of all the multitudinous groups of people in the country, [do] you have to single out the Negroes and give them this separate treatment?

It can't be because of slavery in the past, because there are very few groups in this country that haven't had slavery some place back in the history of their groups. It can't be color, because there are Negroes as white as the drifted snow, with blue eyes, and they are just as segregated as the colored men.

The only thing it can be is an inherent determination that the people who were formerly in slavery, regardless of anything else, shall be kept as near that stage as possible. And now is the time, we submit, that this Court should make clear that that is not what our Constitution stands for.[3]

The Justices were being asked to make law. This was something that Congress is supposed to do. But Congress didn't have the courage to do it. If the Supreme Court ruled that racial segregation was wrong, their ruling would affect twenty-one states (those that supported segregation) and the District of Columbia. Paul Wilson, the assistant attorney general of Kansas, pointed that out. He asked if all those states had been wrong for seventy-five years in believing that separate facilities, though equal, were legal within the meaning of the Fourteenth Amendment.

In response, Justice Burton asked if Wilson didn't think it possible that, during those seventy-five years, the social and economic conditions of the nation might have changed. What might have been a valid interpretation of them seventy-five years ago would not be valid today.

"We recognize that as a possibility," Wilson responded. "We do not believe that the record discloses any such change."

"But that might be a difference between saying that these Courts of Appeal and state supreme courts have been wrong for seventy-five years," Burton added.

"Yes, sir," said Wilson. "We concede that this Court can overrule the *Plessy* doctrine [which established the separate but equal concept], but nevertheless, until it is overruled, it is the best guide we have."

At that point, Justice Frankfurter broke into the conversation. "As I understood by brother Burton's question or as I got the implication of his question, it was not that the Court would have to overrule those [separate but equal] cases; the Court would simply have to recognize that laws are kinetic, and some new things have happened, not deeming those decisions wrong, but bringing into play new situations toward a new decision."

"We agree with that proposition," said Wilson, "but, I repeat, we do not think that there is anything in the record here that would justify such a conclusion."[4]

After several more minutes of arguments, the Court adjourned for the day. They would continue, the following morning, a line of questioning concerning the other cases being presented along with *Brown*. Following Marshall's concluding remarks, Davis, the gray-haired former solicitor general, former ambassador to Great Britain, and noted constitutional lawyer, stood up. Davis picked up on a previous question to Marshall. He emphasized that, if the states were forbidden to discriminate in their schools on the basis of race, they would also be forbidden to segregate its pupils on the ground of sex, age, or mental ability.

Davis then made an unpardonable mistake. He told the Justices how they must think.

"It is the duty of the Court," he said, to interpret the Fourteenth Amendment by placing the Court "as nearly as possible in the condition of those who framed the instrument [Constitution]."

Justice Burton, sounding somewhat irritated, replied, "But the Constitution is a living document that must be interpreted in relation to the facts of the time in which it is interpreted."

Davis replied by saying that circumstances may change within the time span of a century. However, he claimed that these circumstances did not alter, expand, or change the language that the framers of the Constitution originally used. Davis then went on to quote a magazine article by Mississippi editor Hodding Carter that justified the continuation of school segregation.

When it was once again Marshall's turn to speak, he spoke about Davis's reference to the article.

"The article quoted was of a newspaperman answering another newspaperman. I know of nothing further removed from scientific work than one newspaperman answering another," he said.

Frankfurter rocked forward in his seat and replied, "I am not going to take issue with you on that."[5]

Later that day, Justice Reed asked Marshall if the lawyer couldn't accept the proposition that segregation in the schools was legislated "to avoid racial friction."

> I know of no Negro legislator in any of these states, Marshall replied, so the people disadvantaged have had no say in this policy. . . . I know that in the South, where I spent most of my time, you will see white and colored kids going down the road together to school. They separate and go to different schools, and they come out and play together. I do not see why there would necessarily be any trouble if they went to school together.[6]

Reed then commented that the question of segregation

was more a matter for the legislature than for the Supreme Court. Marshall expressed his disagreement. He insisted that the rights of minorities were protected not by the legislature, but by the courts.

With that, the arguments ended and the Justices filed out of the courtroom. Marshall admitted later that he did not believe he had swayed the five Justices he needed to his side.

While they were waiting, the press presented the case to its readers as few cases had been presented before, and for good reason. As *Brown* had unfolded in the Court, millions of Americans were suddenly exposed through newspaper and magazine articles and radio and television newscasts to a wide range of bizarre laws they had not known existed. Among them:

- Florida and North Carolina required that textbooks used by blacks and whites be stored separately and must never be mixed together.

- Oklahoma required that separate telephone booths for blacks and whites be provided.

- Louisiana and South Carolina required separate black and white seating at circuses.

- Mississippi prohibited anyone from printing or circulating printed matter in favor of social equality or interracial marriages.

- Alabama, Mississippi, and South Carolina required black nurses for black patients in hospitals and white nurses for white patients.

- Alabama, Arkansas, Florida, Georgia, and North and South Carolina prohibited chaining black and white prisoners together.

As time went on, the NAACP received tons of mail supporting its handling of the *Brown* case. Win or lose, one thing was clear. The question of segregation was before the American public as it had never been before. Finally, in June 1953, the Court met to announce its decision. Marshall learned that the Court was requesting additional information on the school segregation cases. The cases would have to be reargued the following fall.

Marshall blamed Chief Justice Vinson for the delay. Vinson, he was sure, was against integration, against voting down decades of "separate but equal." So long as the Chief Justice had his say, it was unlikely that the remaining Justices would go against him. Marshall thought about Vinson and his pending decision every day. He wondered just how the Chief Justice would vote.

But before Vinson had the chance to do so, something happened that would change the makeup of the Court. On the evening of September 8, 1953, Vinson told his wife that his stomach was bothering him. A few hours later, he died, the victim of a heart attack.

With an unexpected opening on the Supreme Court, President Dwight D. Eisenhower nominated California governor Earl Warren to be the new Chief Justice. Warren, like Eisenhower, was known to favor integration. Eisnehower was known to support a "slow, easy" move away from segregation. Warren's exact position on how and when to implement integration wasn't clear. A total of nine Justices were once again seated on the bench, and reargument of the case began on December 7, 1953. The Supreme Court building was filled with spectators. Presenting arguments for the states were not only Davis, the renowned constitutionalist, but also T. Justin Moore and Attorney General J. Lindsay Almond, two of the

United States Supreme Court Chief Justice Fred M. Vinson was a
conservative sixty-two-year-old Kentuckian. He had been appointed to the
Court by Harry S. Truman. His unexpected death in 1953 would change
the face of the Court.

most prestigious lawyers the state of Virginia had ever produced. Marshall anchored the case for *Brown*.

After two days of passionate arguments both for and against segregation in the schools, the Court adjourned. The fate of segregation in the schools was now totally in the hands of the Justices.

Marshall was ailing at the time, as much from the neglect of his health from years of overwork as anything. He failed to pay much attention to his body's warnings because he was so consumed by his commitment to the NAACP.

On March 17, 1954, at 12:52 P.M., Chief Justice Warren entered the courtroom and picked up a document from the bench. He announced that the judgment and opinion of the Court in the case of *Brown* v. *Board of Education of Topeka, Kansas* had been reached.

As the journalists who had been waiting in the press room rushed back into Court, Warren read the decision:

> In approaching this problem, we cannot turn the clock back to . . . 1896 when *Plessy* v. *Ferguson* was written. We must consider public education in the light of its full development and its present place in American life throughout the Nation. Only in this way can it be determined if segregation in public schools deprives these plaintiffs of the equal protection of the laws.
>
> Today, education is perhaps the most important function of state and local governments. Compulsory school attendance laws and the great expenditures for education both demonstrate our recognition of the importance of education to our democratic society. It is required in the performance of our most basic public responsibilities, even service in the armed forces. It is the very foundation of good citizenship.

We come then to the question presented: Does segregation of children in public schools solely on the basis of race, even though the physical facilities and other "tangible" factors may be equal, deprive the children of the minority group of equal educational opportunities? We believe that it does.

. . . To separate them from others of similar age and qualifications solely because of their race generates a feeling of inferiority as to their status in the community that may affect their hearts and minds in a way unlikely ever to be undone. The effect of this separation on their educational opportunities was well stated by a finding in the Kansas case by a court which nevertheless felt compelled to rule against the Negro plaintiffs.

Segregation of white and colored children in public schools has a detrimental effect upon the colored children. The impact is greater when it has the sanction of the law; for the policy of separating the races is usually interpreted as denoting the inferiority of the Negro group. A sense of inferiority affects the motivation of a child to learn. Segregation with the sanction of law, therefore, has a tendency to [retard] the educational and mental development of Negro children and to deprive them of some of the benefits they would receive in a racial[ly] integrated school system.

Whatever may have been the extent of psychological knowledge at the time of *Plessy* v. *Ferguson*, this finding is amply supported by modern authority. Any language in *Plessy* v. *Ferguson* contrary to this finding is rejected.

We conclude that in the field of public education the doctrine of "separate but equal" has no place. Separate educational facilities are inherently unequal.

> Therefore, we hold that the plaintiffs and others similarly situated for whom the actions have been brought are, by reason of the segregation complained of, deprived of the equal protection of the laws guaranteed by the Fourteenth Amendment.[7]

The spectators in the courtroom sat silent for several moments. It seemed an eternity before anyone could work up the courage to break the silence—to say something or applaud or even to shift in their seats. Finally, Marshall turned to one of his fellow lawyers and said they'd hit the jackpot.

He had just won a *unanimous* decision from the nation's highest court—a decision destined to change the shape and destiny of America. In later years, when recalling the *Brown* case, Warren would comment about the strange course the arguments had taken during the case:

> One might expect, as I did, that the lawyers representing black schoolchildren would appeal to the emotions of the Court based upon their many years of oppression, and that the states would hold to strictly legal matters. More nearly the opposite developed. Thurgood Marshall made no emotional appeal, and argued the legal issues in a rational manner as cold as steel. On the other hand, states' attorney Davis, a great advocate and orator, former Democratic candidate for the presidency of the United States, displayed a great deal of emotion, and on more than one occasion broke down and took a few moments to compose himself.[8]

The unanimous 1954 decision left little doubt in anyone's mind. Despite the outcome of *Brown*, the battle was not yet over, however. There would be battles in Jackson, Mississippi, riots in Selma, Alabama, and boycotts in Memphis, Tennessee. Some southern public-school officials had vowed

Marshall's wife Buster died in 1955. He eventually married again, this time to Cecilia Suyat (shown here). They had two sons together.

that blood would run in the streets of their towns before even one southern white girl would be allowed to attend school with overgrown Negro males.

But those were threats yet to be seen. For now, Marshall and the NAACP had won a major victory. They had secured the right of a young girl from Kansas to attend the school of her choice.

But there was heartache ahead for Marshall. His beloved wife, Buster, who became ill in late 1953, died early in 1955, leaving a hole in Marshall's heart. He eventually filled the void by marrying Cecilia Suyat of Hawaii—"Cissy," as Marshall called her. The couple had two sons. The first was named Thurgood, Jr.; the second, John.

Problems from the South

In 1952, while working on the *Brown* case, Marshall was basking in the glow of tremendous success in other areas. He had forced the South to change some of its segregated ways. He had been the key in forcing the University of Maryland to accept African-American law student Donald Murray. He had masterminded the plan to get the University of Oklahoma to admit G. W. McLaurin and Ada Sipuel. He also helped in requiring the University of Texas to admit Heman Sweatt. All across the land, it appeared that Americans were experiencing a new era of integration and social progress. But this was not to be.

On September 20, 1952, two young African-American women, Autherine Lucy and Polly Myers, attempted to register for classes at the University of Alabama in Tuscaloosa. The two were told that a mistake had been made. The university did not admit Negroes.

Lucy and Myers called the NAACP, which took the case to the United States District Court in Birmingham. Judge Hobart Grooms ruled that the university had to admit African Americans. But the university was not yet convinced that it had lost the battle. Lawyers for the institution used extraordinary stalling tactics. It wasn't until October of 1955 that the Supreme Court of the United States enforced Judge Grooms's order.

On January 31, 1956, university officials notified Lucy that she could register. Myers was told that the trustees were rejecting her application because "her conduct and marital record have been such she does not meet the admission standards of the University."[1] No one was quite sure what that meant. But obviously university officials were not yet ready to give in.

On February 1, 1956, Lucy was met by Dean of Women Sarah Healy. She took the young African-American woman into her office, put her through a special registration program, and informed her that she would not be given a room in a dormitory or be allowed to eat in the cafeteria. The next day, Lucy attended class. She was the only African-American student in a student body of thousands. That night, about twelve hundred university students assembled around a burning cross. They set off firecrackers, and shouted slogans about keeping Alabama white.

On February 5, Lucy arrived at Smith Hall only to find some fifty white workers from a nearby foundry waiting for her. They threw eggs and rocks, chasing Lucy and Dean Healy across the campus and shouting "Lynch the nigger!"[2]

When university officials asked Governor James Folsom to call out the National Guard, the governor refused. He said that it was normal for different races not to get along with one another.

The next day, citing potential danger to Lucy, the university banned her until further notice. On February 9, NAACP lawyers asked Judge Grooms to order the university to readmit Lucy. But, the NAACP made a fatal legal mistake. The civil rights group claimed that university officials had intentionally plotted to have the mob create an atmosphere of danger. This would give the university an excuse for expelling Lucy. University lawyers naturally denied the charges as untrue and outrageous. University officials then expelled Lucy because, they claimed, she had made false charges against the university.

Marshall and the NAACP had suffered a devastating loss. The case of Autherine Lucy was history. But the officials at the University of Alabama weren't the only problem for Marshall in Alabama. On January 14, 1963, a politically savvy man by the name of George Wallace stood on the spot of the Alabama capitol where years earlier Jefferson Davis had taken the oath as president of the Confederacy. Wallace laid his hand on the same Bible that Davis had used, and he said, after taking the oath of office of the governor,

> Today I have stood where Jefferson Davis stood and took an oath to my people. It is very appropriate then, that from this Cradle of the Confederacy, this very heart of the great Anglo-Saxon [white] Southland, that today we sound the drum for freedom as have our generations of forebears before us time and again down through history. Let us rise to the call of the freedom-loving blood that is in us and send our answer to the tyranny that clanks its chains upon the South. . . .
>
> In the name of the greatest people that have ever trod this earth, I draw the line in the dust and toss the gauntlet before the feet of tyranny. And I say: Segregation now! Segregation tomorrow! Segregation forever![3]

By preaching his antiracial message in Alabama, Wallace

knew that he would upset both Marshall and the NAACP. He was convinced, though, that blacks and whites did not belong together. By flexing his political muscles, he intended to convince civil rights groups to keep their hands off Alabama. But Wallace's plan didn't work. Later that year, two twenty-year-old blacks, Vivian Malone and James A. Hood, prepared to register for classes at the University of Alabama. Shortly before their registration, white segregationists bombed the black-owned A. G. Gaston Motel. They also bombed the home of the Reverend A. D. King, the younger brother of the Reverend Martin Luther King, Jr.

Rioting between blacks and whites broke out in Birmingham. President John F. Kennedy took the first steps to call the Alabama National Guard in to stop the bloodshed. Wallace had been governor at the time for only six months. He claimed that, by grabbing control of the powers granted to the governor, Kennedy was taking illegal action for which he had no authority. Wallace was not content to promote the segregationists' cause. He blamed the violence of the previous few weeks on the group nearly everyone in America feared and hated—the Communists!

As a personal show of strength, Wallace said he would go to Tuscaloosa to block the registration of the two black students who intended to attend the university. He ordered a National Guard plane to fly him, several of his aides, and a small group of bodyguards to Tuscaloosa. He called up 500 members of the Alabama National Guard. He would show Kennedy—and the world—that he, not the president, controlled what happened in Alabama. He also called more than 800 highway patrolmen, and he deputized game wardens, revenue agents, and others and ordered them to Tuscaloosa.

On June 9, 1963, fifteen heavily armed white men were

Governor George Wallace of Alabama (left) salutes the commander of the federalized Alabama National Guard, Brigadier General Henry Graham. Troops were sent to the campus of the University of Alabama to enforce court-ordered enrollment of two African-American students. Wallace was trying to prevent their admission.

arrested in Tuscaloosa. They were charged with planning to incite violence. The men were quickly released on bonds posted by Robert M. Shelton. Shelton was the Imperial Wizard of the Ku Klux Klan and a longtime friend of Governor Wallace.

Meanwhile, the Justice Department had sent Deputy Attorney General Nicholas B. Katzenbach, John Doar from the department's civil rights division, and several other federal officials to Tuscaloosa. They were to oversee the registration of Malone and Hood. The next day, on June 10, Kennedy sent a strongly worded telegram to Wallace. He told the governor that his threat to bar students was:

> in defiance of the order of the Alabama Federal District Court and in violation of accepted standards of public conduct. . . . I therefore urgently ask you to consider the consequences to your state and its fine university if you persist in setting an example of defiant conduct, and urge you instead to leave these matters in the courts of law where they belong.[4]

Wallace was not swayed.

When Malone and Hood arrived at Foster Auditorium, accompanied by Katzenbach, several other federal officials, and a group of United States marshals, they were met by Wallace. Wallace was surrounded by his state troopers, standing in the door. Katzenbach asked Wallace four times to stand aside and allow Malone and Hood to enter the auditorium to register. Each time Wallace refused.

Almost five hours later, Kennedy ordered units of the Thirty-first (Dixie) Division to the Tuscaloosa campus under command of Brigadier General Henry V. Graham. The showdown had reached its peak. Outmaneuvered and overpowered, Wallace grudgingly gave way. He allowed the

Governor George Wallace of Alabama (left) blocks U.S. Deputy Attorney General Nicholas B. Katzenbach from entering Foster Auditorium at the University of Alabama. Katzenbach was attempting to enforce enrollment of two African-American students at the school, following a court order.

two African-American students to enter the university under heavy federal guard.

The following Sunday, a bomb exploded in the Sixteenth Street Baptist Church in Birmingham. It killed four young African-American girls and injured dozens of others who had been attending a Bible class. That same day, two other African-American children were killed. The struggle for integration in Alabama, it seemed, was far from over.

During the next few months, George Wallace's reputation as a no-nonsense, gutsy politician who was not afraid to stand up to the federal government continued to grow. He had become so powerful throughout the South that he decided to run for president of the United States.

As Wallace traveled around the country, he talked constantly about the values of restoring law and order to America. Yet few people he spoke to in Michigan, Maryland, or Ohio knew that Alabama had one of the highest crime rates in the nation. He spoke with ease about eliminating corruption in the nation's capital. Yet his own administration had been among the most corrupt of any state in the nation. He talked of ending violence in the streets of America. Yet he continued to support Shelton, the Klan leader. He also used his political influence to protect some of the most ruthless segregationists in Alabama.

When the presidential election was finally held in 1968, Wallace, running as a third-party candidate against Democrat Hubert H. Humphrey and Republican Richard M. Nixon, gathered in nearly ten million votes. This encouraged him to run again four years later.

Wallace's showing in 1972 was nothing short of remarkable. He won early primary elections in Tennessee, Florida, and North Carolina. These were southern states in which he was expected to win. He came in second in Wisconsin, Indiana, and Pennsylvania. He was leading in Maryland and Michigan. He might well have been on his way to the presidency—and to changing the face of racial relations in America forever—when something intervened. Wallace was campaigning in Maryland when a twenty-one-year-old student from Milwaukee asked the governor to come over and shake his hand. As Wallace approached, the man pulled out a .38-caliber revolver and fired four shots into the governor's body. One of the bullets lodged in his spinal column, paralyzing him for life and ending his bid for the presidency.

Wallace was not the only one who took issue with Thurgood Marshall. When President Kennedy announced in 1961 that he was going to appoint Marshall to the Second Circuit Court of Appeals in New York, Marshall's enemies came out of the woodwork. Among the most powerful was Strom Thurmond, the segregationist senator from South Carolina, where racial prejudice and hatred were widespread.

The confirmation hearings on Marshall began in 1961 and dragged on and on. Finally, after more than a year of intensive questioning, the Senate gave Marshall its approval. The new judge took his place on the bench, where he served for three and a half years. During that time, Marshall exhibited the legal brilliance that marked his work as the NAACP's chief attorney. He wrote 118 opinions, not one of which was reversed.

The position of court of appeals judge is a low-profile one. Marshall, however, soon came to the attention of someone who was very impressed with both his qualifications and his legal successes. When President Kennedy was assassinated in 1963, Lyndon B. Johnson took Kennedy's place in the White House. He decided that he wanted

Marshall to become the first African-American Justice on the Supreme Court of the United States.

Johnson was determined that Marshall would not go through the same kind of confirmation hearings the African-American judge had endured when he was being considered for the court of appeals. Johnson had one thing going for him that Kennedy had not. He was a longtime politician who had done a lot of favors for his peers in Congress. Now, Johnson felt, it was time to call those favors in. He had a plan for Thurgood Marshall.

Johnson talked freely about Marshall's credentials as a courtroom lawyer. He described Marshall as a lawyer and judge of high ability, a patriotic American, and a gentleman of spotless integrity. Johnson said that he was making Marshall solicitor general. The position of solicitor general is an important job in the federal government. As solicitor general, Marshall would be the person who decided which of hundreds of government appeals would go before the Supreme Court. He would have a staff of ten of the best lawyers in the country. He would have access to the entire legal staffs of all federal departments and agencies.

After he had argued more cases before the Supreme Court than any other lawyer in America, he would be nominated to be an Associate Justice. Johnson couldn't imagine how anyone could turn him down.

The president took Marshall, at fifty-seven years old, off the U.S. Court of Appeals for the Second Circuit. He then nominated Marshall to be solicitor general of the United States. Thurgood Marshall was the first African American ever to hold that position.

Marshall had struggled for years as a poorly funded, frequently threatened, often hated, and sometimes abused civil rights lawyer. Now he was suddenly free from the limits his former position had placed upon him; and he found that he had all the money he needed. He had the legal support of brilliant attorneys from every corner of the federal government. In the area of civil rights, he could now accomplish in weeks what had formerly taken him years.

In June 1967, President Johnson sent word to Marshall that he wanted to see him. Marshall had heard that Supreme Court Justice Tom Clark had resigned from the Court. A vacancy now existed. Marshall telephoned his wife and told her that he suspected Johnson wanted to nominate him for the vacancy.

Marshall arrived at the White House just as Johnson was ending a meeting with his advisers on the subject of the Vietnam War. When Johnson said he wanted Marshall to be the nation's first African-American Supreme Court Justice, Marshall acted surprised.

"Oh, boy!" he shouted. "Wait till Cissy hears this. Is she ever gonna be shocked!"

"You mean you haven't told her anything?" Johnson replied.

"How could I tell her when nobody's told me anything?" Marshall said.

"Well, . . . let's get her on the speakerphone and we'll all tell her," the president said.

Marshall might have pulled off the pretense except for one thing: Cissy did not realize she had been put on the speakerphone.

"It's me, honey," Marshall said.

"Yeah, honey," Cissy replied. "Did we get the Supreme Court appointment?"[5]

Johnson, who was not especially well known for his sense of humor, rocked back in his chair and roared with laughter.

The next day, Johnson informed the press of his decision:

> I believe it is the right thing to do, the right time to do it, the right man, and the right place. Statisticians tell me that probably only one or two living men have argued as many cases before the [Supreme] Court, and perhaps less than half a dozen in all the history of the nation.[6]

As chief counsel for the National Association for the Advancement of Colored People, Marshall had won twenty-seven of thirty-four cases he argued before the Supreme Court. As U.S. Solicitor General, he had argued the government's case on nineteen occasions and lost only five.

Chief Justice Earl Warren told the press that Marshall's nomination was an excellent choice. Despite support from Johnson and Warren, Marshall's appointment to the Court still had to be confirmed by the Senate. One of the toughest questioners he faced was North Carolina senator Sam Ervin. Ervin was once a judge. He was particularly interested in learning of Marshall's ideas about people using the Fifth Amendment to avoid answering questions in Court.

Marshall responded quite properly. He stated that it was not appropriate for him to comment on issues concerning the Fifth Amendment, since Fifth Amendment cases were likely to come before the Court. That response left the congressman less than satisfied.

> **Ervin:** I will tell you, Judge, if you are not going to answer a question about anything which might possibly come before the Supreme Court some time in the future, I cannot ask you a single question about anything that is relevant to this inquiry.
>
> **Marshall:** All I am trying to say, Senator, is I do not think you want me to be in the position of giving you

Marshall's appointment to the Supreme Court was highly supported by President Lyndon B. Johnson (center). However, the Senate did not prove to be quite as supportive.

a statement on the Fifth Amendment, and then, if I am confirmed and sit on the Court, when a Fifth Amendment case comes up, I will have to disqualify myself.

Ervin: If you have no opinions on what the Constitution means at this time, you ought not to be confirmed. Anybody that has been at the bar as long as you have, and has as distinguished a legal career as you have, certainly ought to have some very firm opinions about the meaning of the Constitution.

Marshall: But as to particular language of a particular section that I know is going to come before the Court, I do have an opinion as of this time. But I think it would be wrong for me to give that opinion at this time. When the case comes before the Court, that will be the time. I say this with all due respect, Senator, that is the only way it has been done before.[7]

Following Ervin's questioning, it was time for Marshall's old foe, Strom Thurmond of South Carolina, to raise objections to Marshall's nomination.

Thurmond: On March eighth, eighteen fifty, Senator Andrew P. Butler, a South Carolina Democrat and a lawyer, who was John C. Calhoun's colleague in the Senate, stated, and I quote: "A free man of color in South Carolina is not regarded as a citizen by her laws but he has high civil rights. His person and property are protected by law, and he can acquire property, and can claim the protection of the laws for their protection . . . but they are persons recognized by law."

Now, do you believe that this passage shows that the State of South Carolina, while a slave state, was the national leader in giving "civil rights" and "protection of the laws" to colored people, or does it show that these terms had a different meaning a century ago than the Supreme Court has recently given them?

Marshall: Well, I don't agree that at that time South Carolina was the leader in giving Negroes their rights.[8]

Several days later, on July 19, 1967, Thurmond went after Marshall with a vengeance. He asked some of the most obscure questions any Supreme Court nominee has ever had to face.

> **Thurmond:** Do you know who drafted the Thirteenth Amendment to the U.S. Constitution?
>
> **Marshall:** No, sir, I don't remember.
>
> **Thurmond:** What constitutional difficulties did Representative John Bingham of Ohio see in congressional enforcement of the privileges and immunities clause of Article Four, section two, through the necessary and proper clause of Article One, section eight?
>
> **Marshall:** I don't understand the question.[9]

Many congressmen and members of the press found Thurmond's line of questioning to be senseless. It went on for hours until finally the senator stepped into a trap that Marshall had been expecting for some time.

> **Thurmond:** What provisions of the slave codes in existence in the South before eighteen sixty was Congress desirous of abolishing by the Civil Rights Bill of eighteen sixty-six?
>
> **Marshall:** Well, as I remember, the so-called Black Codes ranged from a newly freed Negro not being able to own property or vote, to a statute in my home state of Maryland which prevented these Negroes from flying kites.[10]

The entire gallery broke into laughter as Thurmond respectfully turned the line of questioning over to Senator James O. Eastland of Mississippi.

> **Eastland:** Now, you have been in a lot of institutions in the Southern states.
>
> **Marshall:** Yes, sir.
>
> **Eastland:** Are you prejudiced against white people in the South?
>
> **Marshall:** Not at all. I was brought up, what I would say was way up South in Baltimore, Maryland. And I worked for white people all my life until I got in college. And from there most of my practice, of course, was in the South, and I don't know, with the possible exception of one person that I was against in the South, that I have any feeling about them.[11]

All in all, Marshall handled the hearings with dignity and intelligence. He answered the questions placed to him to the best of his ability. He never once shrank from any of the questioning senators.

Marshall had swept through the confirmation hearings in perfect form. Now it was up to the U.S. Senate to determine whether or not the nation would get its first African-American Supreme Court Justice.

Justice Marshall

Thurgood Marshall had walked through the massive bronze doors of the Supreme Court building—one of the most majestic buildings in Washington, D.C.—many times before. But never before had he walked in as a Supreme Court Justice. He prepared to take his place in history as the first African-American Justice since the Court's founding in 1789. It was an honor, and Marshall intended to do the best job he could.

The man who had fought for more than three decades for civil rights soon found himself in a boiling pot of controversy. But ironically the controversy had nothing to do with civil rights. It had to do instead with rights for women.

Marshall joined the Court in 1967, just two years after the landmark decision of *Griswold* v. *Connecticut.* In this case, the Court had ruled that the state could not interfere in a couple's decision to use contraceptives. The Supreme Court based its decision on the personal freedom granted by the First and Fourteenth amendments.

Now, in 1971, a new landmark case stood before the court. It would become one of the most important and far-reaching cases of Marshall's life. Norma McCorvey was a Texas woman who claimed to have been raped in 1969 while working for a traveling carnival. She sought an abortion to end the pregnancy resulting from the rape. The courts in Texas refused to allow women to have abortions legally. McCorvey, calling herself Jane Roe in order to protect her privacy, decided to file a suit with the Supreme Court of the United States. She would try to overturn the Texas antiabortion laws.

Norma McCorvey's right to have an abortion was at stake, as was the right of women everywhere to have abortions. McCorvey's attorneys, Texans Sarah Weddington and Linda Coffee, were seeking to strike down antiabortion laws everywhere.

Sarah Weddington presented her oral arguments in favor of legalizing abortion to the Court. She was followed by Jay Floyd, a member of the Texas attorney general's office. Floyd's argument centered around the idea that human life begins at the moment of conception. Therefore, he argued, by having an abortion, a woman was committing murder.

Floyd answered several questions from Chief Justice Warren Burger, as well as from several other Justices. Marshall asked Floyd if he could say at what point in a woman's pregnancy life begins.

"At any time, Mr. Justice," said Floyd. "We make no distinction."

"You make no distinction whether there's life or not?" Marshall demanded.

"We say there is life from the moment of impregnation."

"And do you have any scientific data to support that?"

"Well, we begin, Mr. Justice, in our brief, with the development of the human embryo, carrying it through to the development of the fetus, from about seven to nine days after conception."

"Well," Marshall inquired, "what about six days?"

"We don't know," said Floyd.

"But this [Texas abortion] statute goes all the way back to one hour."

Floyd found himself growing increasingly frustrated by Marshall's line of questioning, for which he was unprepared.

"I don't . . . Mr. Justice, there are unanswerable questions in this field, I . . . "

The observers in the courtroom, sensing Floyd's frustration, suddenly broke into laughter. Marshall responded, "I withdraw the question," and the courtroom burst into still more laughter.[1]

With the arguments concluded, the Justices finally adjourned. They met again during the week of December 16, 1971, to discuss *Roe* v. *Wade*. From the start, the discussion ran into problems. Chief Justice Burger seemed to favor upholding the Texas abortion laws. He implied however, that the laws were vague and perhaps even unconstitutional. Justice Marshall—along with Justices William Brennan and William O. Douglas—strongly supported overturning the Texas laws. They supported legalizing abortion. Justice White, on the other hand, was firmly convinced that the Texas laws should remain in effect. He was opposed to abortion.

On December 20, Burger wrote that *Roe* v. *Wade* would probably need to be reargued. The case was scheduled for reargument on October 10, 1972. Following the second hearing, the Justices once again adjourned.

By now Marshall saw that a clear majority of the Court was ready to side with Jane Roe. But it was also clear that Burger had by no means given in to the pressure from his fellow Justices. Marshall watched with amusement the "logrolling" going on. This was his term for one Justice trying to influence another into changing his decision.

Burger finally assigned the task of writing the Court's opinion to Justice Harry A. Blackmun. Blackmun showed his preliminary draft to Justice William Brennan. Brennan responded by writing a forty-eight-page memo of suggestions. Blackmun basically approved of Brennan's suggestions and wrote them into his opinion.

Blackmun then shared his opinion with Burger. Burger was opposed to it. Blackmun, anticipating Burger's opposition, agreed to divide the nine months of pregnancy into three trimesters, or twelve-week periods. During the first trimester, a woman would be allowed to get an abortion without any interference from the state. During the second trimester, the state could permit the abortion, in order to protect the health of the mother. During the third trimester, the state could prevent the abortion in order to save the life of the fetus.

Marshall objected to limiting the availability of abortions to fixed twelve-week periods. How could a poor mother, he asked Blackmun, be restricted to an abortion during so rigid a period of time when she might not be able to afford to see a doctor for fifteen or twenty weeks? What if she lived in a rural community and had no transportation to a hospital or an abortion clinic? Remember, Marshall told Blackmun, that not all pregnant women are middle-income or well-to-do. Many are poor, with few resources.

So, once again, Blackmun went back to the drawing board, changing the wording in his opinion to reflect the more liberal desires of Marshall. One "compelling point [for obtaining an abortion]," Blackmun wrote, "is at approximately the end of the first trimester." By adding the word *approximately,* Blackmun satisfied Marshall's objection to including rigid time periods.

Blackmun then added a section limiting abortions to a period prior to the "viability of the fetus." This meant that abortions would be legal only until the fetus was capable of leaving the mother's womb and surviving. Finally, Blackmun's opinion was approved by the Court, and the Justices released it. In part, it read:

> The Constitution does not explicitly mention any right of privacy. In a line of decisions, however, the Court has recognized that a right of personal privacy, or a guarantee of certain areas or zones of privacy, does exist under the Constitution.

> This right of privacy, whether it be founded in the Fourteenth Amendment's concept of personal liberty and restrictions upon state action, as we feel it is, or, as the District Court determined, [it be founded] in the Ninth Amendment's reservation of rights to the people, [it is] is broad enough to encompass a woman's decision whether or not to terminate her pregnancy.[2]

In discussing the question of when a fetus becomes a "person" in the eyes of the law, Blackmun wrote:

81

The Constitution does not define "person" in so many words. The use of the word is such that it has application only postnatally [after birth]. All this, together with our observation that, throughout the major portion of the nineteenth century, prevailing legal abortion practices were far freer than they are today, persuades us that the word "person," as used in the Fourteenth Amendment, does not include the unborn.

Texas urges that, apart from the Fourteenth Amendment, life begins at conception and is present throughout pregnancy, and that, therefore, the state has a compelling interest in protecting that life from and after conception.

We need not resolve the difficult question of when life begins. When those trained in the respective disciplines of medicine, philosophy, and theology are unable to arrive at any consensus [of when life begins], the judiciary, at this point in the development of man's knowledge, is not in a position to speculate as to the answer.

The unborn have never been recognized in the law as persons in the whole sense.[3]

In writing about the state's role in preventing the "murder" of a young life, Blackmun adopted the points that Marshall had earlier suggested to him:

With respect to the state's important and legitimate interest in potential life, the "compelling" point is at viability. This is so because the fetus then presumably has the capability of meaningful life outside the mother's womb. If the state is interested in protecting fetal life after viability, it may go so far as to proscribe [prevent] abortion during that period except when [the abortion] is necessary to preserve the life or health of the mother.[4]

In the end, seven Justices voted with the majority to strike down Texas's antiabortion laws. Only Justices Byron White and William Rehnquist dissented.

Along with the long-awaited decision of the Court came national notoriety. Pro-life (antiabortion) groups across the country denounced the Court's decision as barbarous. The Catholic Church issued a statement condemning the decision. Letters by the thousands poured into the Supreme Court building. So, too, did death threats. Marshall received more than his share and later commented that he believed most of them had come from organized groups, rather than from concerned individuals.

But not all of Marshall's correspondence was negative. From all over America, he received congratulations for having the courage to overturn this law. It was a law that for years had restricted a woman's right to determine her own future. As a result, Marshall had become an overnight champion of women, both black and white.

Following the controversial decision in *Roe*, Marshall wrote the dissenting opinion for *Poelker* v. *Doe*, which said:

> An unwanted child may be disruptive and destructive of the life of any woman, but the impact is felt most by those too poor to ameliorate [lessen] those effects. If funds for an abortion are unavailable, a poor woman may feel that she is forced to obtain an illegal abortion that poses a serious threat to her health and even her life. . . . If she refuses to take this risk and undergoes the pain and danger of state-financed pregnancy and childbirth, she may well give up all chance of escaping the cycle of poverty. [Without]

day-care facilities, she will be forced into full-time child care for years to come; she will be unable to work so that her family can break out of the welfare system or the lowest income brackets. If she already has children, another infant to feed and clothe may well stretch the budget past the breaking point.

On the subject of what happens to unwanted children, Marshall also said:

> The enactments challenged here brutally [force] poor women to bear children whom society will scorn for every day of their lives. Many thousands of unwanted minority and mixed-race children now spend blighted lives in foster homes, orphanages, and "reform" schools. . . . Many children of the poor, sadly, will attend second-rate segregated schools. . . . And opposition remains strong against increasing Aid to Families with Dependent Children [welfare] benefits for impoverished mothers and children, so that there is little chance for the children to grow up in a decent environment. I am appalled at the ethical bankruptcy of those who preach a "right to life" that means, under present social policies, a bare existence in utter misery for so many poor women and their children.[5]

As the 1960s gave way to the 1970s, Marshall's earlier work with the NAACP began to pay off. Many Americans of all races now supported the Court's recent decisions that showed that African Americans and other long-suffering minorities should be given special treatment. This would help them to fit into the mainstreams of American society. Why, people wondered, had the Alabama State Highway Patrol never had a single African-American patrolman in the history of the state? Why did many southern colleges and universities have so few African Americans and other minorities on their faculties? It seemed only right that "affirmative action" programs be promoted. Affirmative action programs were designed to show preference to minorities to make up for discrimination in the past.

However, in the late 1970s and early 1980s, a number of lawsuits challenging affirmative action began appearing in court. White parents suddenly began objecting when colleges such as Stanford and Cornell began giving scholarships to blacks instead of whites. Whites were being rejected even though they scored higher on their tests than blacks. White policemen and firemen objected when blacks with less seniority were promoted over whites in order to equalize the number of whites and minorities in supervisory positions.

Suddenly the benefits of affirmative action didn't seem quite so clear to white America, especially when a job, a promotion, a raise, a scholarship, or something else of value was at stake.

The backlash against affirmative action finally reached the Supreme Court—and Thurgood Marshall—in 1978. A white student by the name of Allan Bakke had sued the University of California, claiming that he had been denied entry to the university's medical school in favor of less qualified black applicants.

The Supreme Court ruled 5 to 4 in favor of Bakke. It ordered the University of California to discontinue its policy of establishing a quota for black applicants. When Justice Powell cast the deciding vote, declaring that the use of quotas to benefit black students was unconstitutional, Marshall fired off an angry dissent:

> While I applaud the judgment of the Court that a university may consider race in its admissions process, it is more than a little ironic that, after several hundred years of class-based discrimination against

The negative side of affirmative action reached the Supreme Court—and Thurgood Marshall—in 1978, when Allan Bakke, a white student, sued the University of California. He claimed he had been denied entry to the university's medical school in favor of less qualified black applicants.

Negroes, the Court is unwilling to hold that a class-based remedy for that discrimination [affirmative action] is permissible. . . .

It is because of a legacy of unequal treatment that we now must permit the institutions of this society to give consideration to race in making decisions about who will hold the positions of influence, affluence, and prestige in America. For far too long, the doors to those positions have been shut to Negroes.[6]

Marhsall pointed out to his fellow Justices that Lyndon B. Johnson, the man who had appointed him to the Supreme Court, once said in a commencement address to the students of Howard University:

You do not take a person who for years has been hobbled by chains and liberate him, bring him up to the starting line of a race, and then say, you're free to compete with all the others.

Negroes are trapped, as many whites are trapped, in inherited gateless poverty. They lack training and skills. They are shut in slums without decent medical care. . . . We are trying to attack these evils. . . .

Much of the Negro community is buried under a blanket of history and circumstance. It is not a lasting solution to lift just one corner of the blanket.[7]

Marshall was determined to work harder than ever to bring freedom to all Americans everywhere—regardless of their race, social standing, or economic condition. He became more dedicated than ever to championing the First Amendment. This guarantees Americans numerous personal freedoms, not the least of which is freedom of speech.

But for Marshall, freedom of speech went far beyond the spoken word. To him, it meant all kinds of expression—from picketing and sit-ins to males wearing long hair and marching against the war in Vietnam. Wherever personal expressions were made in public forums, Marshall believed, those expressions were protected by the First Amendment. He felt this was true even when it came to the military, which for decades the Court had considered separate from the rest of American society. Marshall believed a person's right to freedom of speech prevailed. In the *Pentagon Papers* case, he defended the right of *The New York Times* and the *Washington Post* to print information the newspapers had received concerning the United States's involvement in Vietnam.

When asked if he felt that the nation's press was the best defense the people had against the government lying to or misleading them, Marshall replied somberly that it is all we have.

Indeed, Marshall understood that a free press is as valuable to a society as the greatest laws designed to protect them. Without a free press, a nation is left with an unrestrained government. Without a free press, a nation full of rich and influential people may quickly learn to play by any rules they choose. To Marshall, that meant that, once again, the poor, the weak, and the minorities would have to bear the suffering.

As his time on the bench passed, it became increasingly clear to courtroom observers that Marshall loved taking the side of the "little people." He would side with the people who lacked power and prestige and needed the protection of the Court even more, at times, than the wealthy and the powerful—even if it meant disagreeing with a majority of his fellow Justices.

"I love a dissent," Marshall once said. "You have to get real mad to write a good dissent. . . . When young lawyers apply to clerk in my office, the first thing I ask is, 'Do you like writing dissents? If you don't, baby, this is not the office for *you*."[8]

To his advantage, Marshall wasn't alone. His longtime colleague and friend, William J. Brennan, also loved to champion the poor and the defenseless. He too would write stirring dissents whenever called for. In fact, Brennan joined Marshall in voting in nearly 95 percent of all cases heard before the Court. This was a greater percentage of agreement than between any other two Justices.

In a way, the friendship and professional respect that developed between Brennan and Marshall was not surprising. Although one was black and the other white, they shared much of the same morality and experiences of youth.

Brennan was born on April 25, 1906, two years before Marshall. Brennan's father, an Irish immigrant, started work as a coal shoveler in Newark, New Jersey. He slowly worked his way up to become a labor leader and, finally, an elected city official. Like Marshall's father, Brennan's believed that education was the key to his son's success. "He was quite a disciplinarian," Brennan once said, "and his absolute determination was that each of us [children] would get everything in the way of an education."[9]

Also like Marshall, Brennan graduated from law school, and then worked his way through various legal positions. Brennan was finally nominated to the Supreme Court by President Dwight D. Eisenhower.

Brennan accepted the nomination eagerly and was quick to endorse Eisenhower's public statement that he chose Brennan because he was "the best man available."

"I was willing to stop the inquiries right there," Brennan once joked.[10]

As the least conservative Justice on the Warren Court, Brennan sat with fellow liberals Hugo Black and William O. Douglas. Later, they would be joined by Arthur Goldberg, Abe Fortas, and Thurgood Marshall. The friendship that Marshall shared with Brennan would last the rest of their lives. It was overshadowed only by Marshall's own sense of independence and wry sense of humor.

Marshall loved entertaining his fellow Justices with stories of the "good old days," when he stood face-to-face with racism and injustice in the deep South. He told of arriving in one southern town only to learn that his client had been lynched earlier that day. He recalled standing on a train platform next to a Southern sheriff who told the attorney in no uncertain terms: "The sun never set on a nigger in this town."[11] Nor did it have a chance to set on Marshall. He caught the next train northward.

Once Marshall told Justice Sandra Day O'Connor a story about a young black man named George Crawford. Crawford had been indicted by an all-white grand jury for murdering a maid and her white employer, who was from a well-to-do Virginia family. Marshall and Charles Houston, acting in Crawford's defense, did everything they could to secure the young man's freedom. They even challenged the fact that no African Americans were present on the jury.

In the end, the jury found Crawford guilty and sentenced him to life in prison. "You know something is wrong with the government's case," Marshall told O'Connor, "when a Negro only gets life for murdering a white woman."[12]

Following the trial, the press asked if Crawford planned to appeal the ruling based on the fact that there were no African Americans on the jury. Marshall recalled the rest of the story to O'Connor: Crawford said, "Mr. Houston, if I have another trial and I get life this time, could they kill me the next time?" Houston told him yes. So Crawford told Houston, "Tell them the defense rests."[13]

Like most of Thurgood Marshall's stories, this one had a message. After years of struggling to win their freedom, African Americans still suffered the injustices and savagery of racism. That's something that Marshall never forgot—and never stopped fighting. His love for championing the underdog would often surface over the years. Time after time, he would go face to face with some of the most powerful people in America. In the process, he would make many political enemies. This never seemed to bother him. It couldn't. More than half a century earlier, his father had told him to do what was right: To live his life as he believed, not as others felt he should.

They were words that would serve Marshall well, words he would never forget.

Changing Times

In his long years of work as the nation's first African-American Supreme Court Justice, Marshall made many historic contributions of great importance to society. He voted against the majority in the affirmative-action case of *Regents of the University of California* v. *Bakke*, saying in his dissent:

> I agree with the judgment of the Court only insofar as it permits a university to consider the race of an applicant in making admissions decisions. I do not agree that petitioner's [the university's] admissions program violates the Constitution. For it must be remembered that, during most of the past 200 years, the Constitution as interpreted by this Court did not prohibit the most ingenious and pervasive forms of discrimination against the Negro. Now, when a State acts to remedy the effects of that legacy of discrimination, I cannot believe that this same Constitution stands as a barrier. . . .

It is because of a legacy of unequal treatment that we now must permit the institutions of this society to give consideration to race in making decisions about who will hold the positions of influence, affluence, and prestige in America. For far too long, the doors to those positions have been shut to Negroes. If we are ever to become a fully integrated society, one in which the color of a person's skin will not determine the opportunities available to him or her, we must be willing to take steps to open those doors.[1]

In the area of capital punishment, Marshall played a key role in overturning the death penalty in the landmark case, *Furman* v. *Georgia.* He firmly believed that death should not be used as punishment. When it came time to vote with the narrowest of majorities, Marshall, in the landmark 5-to-4 decision, said in his own opinion: "In *Furman,* I concluded that the death penalty is constitutionally invalid for two reasons. First, the death penalty is excessive. And second, the American people, fully informed as to the purposes of the death penalty and its liabilities, would in my view reject it as morally unacceptable."[2]

In the area of First Amendment rights, Marshall sided with the majority in *New York Times* v. *United States.* He offered some interesting comments. In the process, he voted down the government's attempt—and that of President Richard M. Nixon—to prevent the nation's press from publishing accurate accounts of the ongoing war in Vietnam.

Either the Government has the power under statutory grant to use traditional criminal law to protect the country [from newspapers printing information] or, if there is no basis for arguing that Congress has made the activity a crime, it is plain that Congress has specifically refused to grant the authority the

Government seeks from this Court. In either case this Court does not have authority to grant the requested relief [of censoring the press]. It is not for this Court to fling itself into every breach perceived by some Government official, nor is it for this Court to take on itself the burden of enacting law, especially a law that Congress has refused to pass.[3]

Marshall went on to address the secondary issue in that case. He spoke of the separation of governmental powers—the executive, the legislative, and the judicial branches:

The Constitution provides that Congress shall make laws, the President execute laws, and the courts interpret laws. . . . It did not provide for government by injunction in which the courts and the Executive can "make law" without regard to the action of Congress. . . .

. . . it is clear that Congress has specifically rejected passing legislation that would have clearly given the President the power he seeks here and made the current activity of the newspapers unlawful. When Congress specifically declines to make conduct unlawful, it is not for this Court to re-decide those issues—to overrule Congress.[4]

In the area of freedom of expression—another one of the guarantees granted by the First Amendment—Marshall was equally clear as to where he stood. *Procunier* v. *Martinez* dealt with the right of prison officials to read inmates' mail. Marshall wrote in a concurring opinion:

The First Amendment serves not only the needs of the polity [government] but also those of the human spirit—a spirit that demands self-expression. Such expression is an integral part of the development of ideas and a sense of identity. To suppress expression is to reject the basic human desire for recognition and affront the individual's worth and dignity. . . . When the prison gates slam behind an inmate, he does not lose his human quality; his mind does not become closed to ideas; his intellect does not cease to feed on a free and open interchange of opinions; his yearning for self-respect does not end; nor is his quest for self-realization concluded. If anything, the needs for identity and self-respect are more compelling in the dehumanizing prison environment. Whether an O. Henry authoring his short stories in a jail cell or a frightened young inmate writing his family, a prisoner needs a medium for self-expression. It is the role of the First Amendment and this Court to protect those precious personal rights by which we satisfy such basic yearnings of the human spirit.[5]

The nation's most outspoken Justice also took a firm, but informed, stand on other key issues of the times. On the issue of abortion he supported a woman's right to determine her own future. On the issue of privacy, he supported people's rights against government intrusion. On the issue of racism, he upheld the idea that all people are created equal. Referring to the Constitution, Marshall insisted that it is a living, changing document open to liberal interpretation. With regard to judicial restraint, he argued that the courts should not interfere where unnecessary.

Asked once which case stood out most in his memory, Marshall replied, "The next [one]. I don't look back, I look forward. And . . . all I know was each job I got was tougher than the one I had before."[6]

Marshall even had a few kind words to say about the conservative Nixon appointee, William H. Rehnquist. Upon Rehnquist's nomination to replace the retiring Earl Warren as

Chief Justice, Marshall commented, "I don't agree with him on much, but he's a great guy."[7]

Marshall once boasted that his job would not be finished so long as there were a breath in his body. By the late 1980s, though, he began to think twice. He started to consider retirement.

Not that Marshall felt his work on the Court was finished. On the contrary, he always reacted to his courtroom labors as if his task had only begun. Still, the time had come. Earl Warren was gone. The replacement nominees of Reagan and Bush were moving toward a greater degree of conservatism. It was time for Marshall to leave.

The man who had made a career out of championing the rights of the minority finally announced his retirement from the Supreme Court on June 29, 1991. He had spent twenty-four years as one of the most powerful men in America.

"I'm old," he said simply, "and falling apart."[8]

There are those who say Marshall was not falling apart so much as he was becoming disillusioned. The exuberance and energy he had in his youth—two ingredients so necessary to fight the evils and wrongdoings of society—had long since gone from him. There was nothing left inside with which he could fight.

At a dedication in his honor at the Howard University School of Law, an aging, pained, eighty-two-year-old Thurgood Marshall, addressed the students with some sadness. "In many facets of life, we are going backwards as a race of people and a nation," he said. "Progress has slowed down. Indeed, it might have stopped."[9]

Despite his sad mood, the crowd cheered him enthusiastically. School officials had not invited the public to the event, but they had sent invitations to the members of the

At the time of his retirement, according to some, Marshall no longer had
the energy of his youth. That youthful energy shows on a younger
Marshall's face (center) following the Supreme Court's declaration that
segregation in public schools was unconstitutional.

Court. Rehnquist, Scalia, and Stevens all sent their regrets. For a while, it appeared as though none of Marshall's fellow Justices would show up. Then, as the ceremony began, they began filing in. First Byron White, then Sandra Day O'Connor, David Souter, Harry Blackmun, and Anthony Kennedy. All came to center stage to honor one of the greatest Supreme Court Justices in history.

Surprised to see so many of his peers in attendance, Marshall looked out among them and quipped, "We have enough Justices to decide a case."[10]

By the following spring, Marshall's health had deteriorated sharply. His eyesight was failing, his legs no longer worked the way they once did, and his breath came in short wispy gasps. Yet, he never lost his sense of humor.

Marshall attended the premier showing of an ABC-TV miniseries, *Separate but Equal.* The tall, distinguished actor Sidney Poitier played attorney Thurgood Marshall. Marshall greeted Poitier as "my twin brother." Asked after the event what he thought of Poitier's portrayal of himself, Marshall said, "He was better than me."[11]

In a tribute to Thurgood Marshall published by the *Stanford University Law Review* in June 1992, Chief Justice Warren E. Burger said of Marshall: "I find it difficult to identify a single individual in the legal profession who has done more to advance the cause of civil rights in this century than Thurgood Marshall."[12]

Associate Justice Byron R. White, in the same tribute, said, "All of us should be very grateful to Thurgood for what he accomplished. . . . There is no doubt that had he never become a judge, he would still be remembered as one of the giants of the law."[13]

Associate Justice Lewis F. Powell, Jr. commented on

Marshall's long and successful career in fighting discrimination while working within the guidelines of the law. Powell had this to say:

> Perhaps because I am a lawyer, I admire Thurgood Marshall as much for how he advanced racial equality as for what he accomplished. Thurgood Marshall steadfastly chose the courts as the avenue by which he sought to change our society. . . . My hope is that one legacy . . . of Thurgood Marshall's unique career will be a sustaining belief in the promise that the . . . law assures protection of the liberties we enjoy. That promise, after all, was never more clearly fulfilled than through Thurgood Marshall's landmark Supreme Court victories.[14]

Associate Justice Anthony M. Kennedy commented on the continuing influence of Supreme Court Justices after they leave the bench:

> As the law unfolds, will Thurgood's voice continue to be heard? I think it will. The central meaning of the Supreme Court as an institution is that it consists of more than the nine Justices who are on its bench. The Court includes as well all those former Justices whose voices remain in the conference room. Their voices remain in a formal sense in their written opinions. In this respect, Thurgood stays at the conference table in a powerful way.[15]

The next year, Marshall passed away. Officially, he died of pneumonia and complications from diabetes and a weak heart. He had many other health problems to which his death could also have been attributed. Some would say, though, that he died not so much of physical degeneration as from spiritual exhaustion. He had seen the state of national events that had led to a changing of the guard in the Court. This was a change that resulted, in his eyes, in the Court's shifting from being the stronghold of liberalism it had once been into a symbol of conservatism.

He had simply had enough.

Asked once in an interview how he hoped to be remembered, Marshall replied simply, "That he did what he could with what he had."[16]

Thurgood Marshall certainly did that and more. In the process, he left behind a legacy that has served as a shining light to those following in his footsteps. Thurgood Marshall may be gone, but his zest for life—and the intensity of his belief in human rights—will live on forever.

Chronology

1908—Thurgood Marshall is born to Norma and William Marshall in Baltimore, Maryland.

1930—Marshall graduates with a bachelor's degree from Lincoln University.

1933—Marshall graduates with honors from Howard University Law School. He gains entrance to the Maryland State Bar.

1934—Marshall begins work as an attorney with the National Association for the Advancement of Colored People (NAACP).

1936—Marshall begins work as deputy assistant special counsel for the National NAACP.

1938—Marshall is named chief legal officer for the NAACP. He wins first major United States Supreme Court victory with NAACP in *Gaines* v. *University of Missouri.*

1952—Marshall presents opening arguments before the United States Supreme Court in the landmark civil rights case of *Brown* v. *Board of Education of Topeka, Kansas.*

1954—Supreme Court rules in favor of Linda Brown.

1961—President John F. Kennedy announces the appointment of Marshall to the Second Circuit Court of Appeals in New York.

1965—President Lyndon B. Johnson appoints Marshall as solicitor general.

1967—President Johnson announces his nomination of Marshall as the first African-American Justice on the Supreme Court. Marshall's nomination to the Supreme Court is confirmed by the Senate.

1971–1973—Marshall participates in landmark abortion decision, *Roe* v. *Wade*; also participates in landmark freedom of the press decision, *New York Times* v. *United States* (1971).

1972—Marshall participates in landmark death penalty case, *Furman* v. *Georgia.*

1974—Marshall participates in landmark executive privilege case, *United States* v. *Nixon.*

1978—Marshall participates in landmark reverse discrimination case, *Regents of the University of California* v. *Bakke.*

1983—Marshall participates in landmark personal rights case, *Immigration and Naturalization Service* v. *Chadha.*

1986—Marshall participates in landmark homosexuality rights case, *Bowers* v. *Hardwick.*

1990—Marshall participates in landmark right-to-die case, *Cruzan* v. *Missouri.*

1991—Marshall retires from the Supreme Court on June 27.

1993—Thurgood Marshall dies at the age of eighty-four.

Chapter Notes

Chapter 1

1. Michael D. Davis & Hunter R. Clark, *Thurgood Marshall: Warrior at the Bar, Rebel on the Bench* (New York: Birch Lane Press, 1992), p. 41.
2. *Colliers Encyclopedia*, February 23, 1952, v.15, p. 230.
3. Glen M. Darbyshire, "Clerking for Justice Marshall," *ABA Journal*, September 1991, p. 51.
4. Karen S. Schneider, Marilyn Balamaci, Katy Kelly, and Deborah Papier, "A Warrior Retires," *People*, July 15, 1991, p. 34.
5. Ibid.
6. Roger Wilkins, "Thurgood and Me," *Mother Jones*, November/December 1991, p. 13.
7. *Ebony*, September 1991, p. 115.

Chapter 2

1. *Time*, December 21, 1953.
2. Carl T. Rowan, *Dream Makers, Dream Breakers, The World of Thurgood Marshall* (New York: Little, Brown, 1993), p. 44.
3. David G. Savage, *Turning Right: The Making of the Rehnquist Supreme Court* (New York: John Wiley & Sons, 1992), pp. 75-76.
4. Rowan, p. 35.
5. Ibid.
6. Savage, p. 76.
7. Rowan, p. 38.
8. Ibid.
9. Ibid., p. 39.
10. Lisa Aldred, *Thurgood Marshall* (New York: Chelsea House Publishers, 1990), p. 36.
11. Rowan, p. 46.
12. Michael D. Davis & Hunter R. Clark, *Thurgood Marshall:*

Warrior at the Bar, Rebel on the Bench (New York: Birch Lane Press, 1992) p. 81.

13. Ibid., p. 79.

14. Rowan, p. 49.

Chapter 3

1. Resolution of the Board of Curators, University of Missouri, March 27, 1936.

2. Carl T. Rowan, *Dream Makers, Dream Breakers: The World of Thurgood Marshall* (New York: Little, Brown, 1993), pp. 72-73.

3. *Gaines* v. *University of Missouri*, Supreme Court of the United States Opinion, December 12, 1938, pp. 1-2.

Chapter 4

1. Michael D. Davis & Hunter R. Clark, *Thurgood Marshall: Warrior at the Bar, Rebel on the Bench* (New York: Birch Lane Press, 1982), p. 112.

2. Carl T. Rowan, *Dream Makers, Dream Breakers: The World of Thurgood Marshall* (New York: Little, Brown, 1993), p. 90.

Chapter 5

1. Michael D. Davis & Hunter R. Clark, *Thurgood Marshall: Warrior at the Bar, Rebel on the Bench* (New York: Birch Lane Press, 1982), p. 139.

2. *Sipuel* v. *Board of Regents of the University of Oklahoma*, 332 U.S. 631 (1948).

3. *McLaurin* v. *Oklahoma State Regents for Higher Education*, 339 U.S. 637 (1950).

4. Davis & Clark, p. 126.

5. Ibid., pp. 128-129.

6. Ibid.

Chapter 6

1. *Brown* v. *Board of Education of Topeka, Kansas*, Supreme Court of the United States Oral Arguments, 347 U.S. 438 (1954).

2. Ibid.

3. Ibid.

4. Ibid.
5. Ibid.
6. Ibid.
7. Ibid.
8. Earl Warren, *The Memoirs of Chief Justice Earl Warren* (Garden City, N.Y.: Doubleday, 1977), p. 287.

Chapter 7
1. Carl T. Rowan, *Dream Makers, Dream Breakers: The World of Thurgood Marshall* (New York: Little, Brown, 1993), p. 253.
2. Ibid.
3. George Wallace, Oath of Office, State of Alabama, January 14, 1963.
4. Ibid.
5. Rowan, pp. 296–297.
6. Senate Judiciary Committee, Confirmation Hearings, July 19, 1967.
7. Ibid.
8. Ibid.
9. Ibid.
10. Ibid.
11. Ibid.

Chapter 8
1. *Roe* v. *Wade*, Supreme Court of the United States Oral Arguments, No. 70-18 (October 11, 1972), pp. 14–15.
2. *Roe* v. *Wade*, Supreme Court of the United States Opinion (January 22, 1973), pp. 1–3.
3. Ibid., p. 4.
4. Ibid., p. 5.
5. *Poelker* v. *Doe*, Supreme Court of the United States Opinion (1977).
6. *University of California Regents* v. *Bakke*, Supreme Court of the United States, Thurgood Marshall dissent (1978).
7. Ibid.
8. Lisa Aldred, *Thurgood Marshall* (New York: Chelsea House Publishers, 1990), p. 147.

9. David G. Savage, *Turning Right: The Making of the Rehnquist Supreme Court* (New York: John Wiley & Sons, 1992), p. 124.

10. Ibid., p. 125.

11. Ibid., p. 78.

12. "Tribute to Justice Thurgood Marshall," *Stanford Law Review*, vol. 44, no. 1217, June 1992, p. 5.

13. Ibid.

Chapter 9

1. *Regents of the University of California* v. *Bakke*, (Opinion of Justice Marshall, June 28, 1978), pp. 1–2.

2. *New York Times Company, et al.* v. *United States of America*, (Opinion of Justice Marshall, June 30, 1971), p. 2.

3. Ibid.

4. Ibid., p. 3.

5. *Procunier* v. *Martinez* (Opinion of Justice Marshall, Aug. 3, 1974), p. 3.

6. "Q & A," *The Docket Sheet*, vol. 28, no. 2, Fall 1991, pp. 1–8.

7. David G. Savage, *Turning Right: The Making of the Rehnquist Supreme Court* (New York: John Wiley & Sons, 1992), p. 14.

8. Karen S. Schneider, Marilyn Balamaci, Katy Kelly, and Deborah Papier, "A Warrior Retires," *People*, July 15, 1991, p. 34.

9. Savage, p. 399.

10. Ibid.

11. Ibid., p. 400.

12. "Tribute to Justice Marshall," *Stanford Law Review*, vol. 44, no. 1217, June 1992, p. 5.

13. "Tribute to Justice Marshall," *Stanford Law Review*, vol. 44, no. 1215, June 1992, p. 2.

14. "Tribute to Justice Marshall," *Stanford Law Review*, vol. 44, no. 1229, June 1992, p. 7.

15. "Tribute to Justice Marshall," *Stanford Law Review*, vol. 44, no. 1221, June 1992, p. 9.

16. "Q & A," p. 9.

Glossary

amicus curiae—Friend of the Court, or one who gives information to the Court pertaining to some matter of law that is in doubt.

argument—A course of reasoning intended to persuade others to believe the same way.

attorney general—The chief law officer of the federal government and of each state's government.

brief—A written argument used by a lawyer to present the basic facts of the client's case, including a statement of the legal questions involved, the law that the lawyer would like to have applied, and what decision he or she wants from the court.

civil rights—Equal rights for citizens given by laws enacted by civilized communities.

concurring opinion—An opinion that basically agrees with the majority opinion, but that is written to express a different view of the issues, to explain a particular judge's opinion, or to detail a point that a judge wants to point out more specifically than the majority opinion does.

Court of Appeals—A court of review having jurisdiction to reevaluate a law as it applies to a particular case.

decision—A final determination arrived at after consideration. A course of action decided upon.

defendant—A person who defends himself or herself against a suit.

determination—A decision by a court.

dissenting opinion—An opinion that disagrees with the disposition made of a case by the majority court.

hearing—A proceeding in which evidence is placed before the court in order to determine facts and to reach a decision on the basis of that evidence.

indictment—A written accusation, drawn up and submitted to a grand jury by the prosecuting attorney, that charges one or more persons with a crime.

integration—The mixing of whites and blacks.

judgment—The final determination of the rights of the parties to a lawsuit.

majority opinion—An opinion that is held by a majority of the court.

opinion—The reason given for a court's judgment, finding, or conclusion.

petition—A formal written request for a certain thing to be done by a court.

petitioner—One who presents a petition to a court.

plaintiff—The person who initially brings a suit.

segregation—The separation of whites and blacks.

separate but equal doctrine—The belief that separate facilities for whites and blacks are acceptable so long as the facilities are equal.

solicitor general—A person appointed by the president to assist the attorney general in performing legal duties.

writ of mandamus—A court order demanding that something be done.

Further Reading

Aldred, Lisa. *Thurgood Marshall.* New York: Chelsea House Publishers, 1990.

Berger, Raoul. *Congress* v. *The Supreme Court.* New York: Bantam Books, 1973.

Berman, Daniel M. *It Is So Ordered: The Supreme Court on School Segregation.* New York: W. W. Norton, 1966.

Friendly, Fred. W., and Martha J. H. Elliott. *The Constitution: That Delicate Balance.* New York: Random House, 1984.

Lawson, Don. *Landmark Supreme Court Cases.* Hillside, N.J.: Enslow Publishers, 1987.

Powledge, Fred. *Free At Last? The Civil Rights Movement and the People Who Made It.* Boston: Little, Brown, 1979.

Rowan, Carl T. *Braking Barriers: A Memoir.* Boston: Little, Brown, 1991.

_____. *Dream Makers, Dream Breakers: The World of Thurgood Marshall.* Boston: Little, Brown, 1993.

Tribe, Laurence H. *God Save This Honorable Court: How the Choice of Justices Can Change Our Lives.* New York: Random House, 1985.

Weiss, Ann. *The Supreme Court.* Hillside, N.J.: Enslow, 1987.

Woodward, Bob, and Scott Armstrong. *The Brethren: Inside the Supreme Court.* New York: Simon & Schuster, 1979.

Woodward, Bob, and Carl Bernstein. *The Final Days.* New York: Simon and Schuster, 1976.

Index

110

111

Polo Grounds, 21
Powell, Lewis F., Jr., 98, 99
primary elections, 68
Procunier v. *Martinez*, 94

R

Reagan, Ronald, 96
Reed, Stanley, 47, 52
Regents of the University of California v. *Bakke*, 92
Rehnquist, William, 83, 95, 98
Roe, Jane, 78, 80
Roe v. *Wade*, 9, 78– 83
Rogers, Elmer, 30, 31, 32, 33
Roosevelt, Franklin D., 37

S

Sawyer Prison Camp, 30, 32
Scott, Charles, 46
Second Circuit Court of Appeals, 69, 70
Selma, Alabama, 58
"separate but equal," 8, 18–19, 28, 38, 41, 47, 49, 51, 54, 57
Separate but Equal, 98
Shelton, Robert M., 66, 68
Sipuel, Ada, 38, 39, 40, 61
Sixteenth Street Baptist Church, 68
South Carolina, 53, 69, 74, 75
South Korea, 41, 42
Spell, Joseph, 29
St. Louis Dispatch, 27
St. Louis Globe-Democrat, 27
Stanford Law Review, 98
Strubing, Eleanor, 29

Sumner Elementary School, 46
Sweatt, Heman Marion, 39, 61

T

Tennessee, 68
Texas, 28, 78, 79, 83
Thurmond, Strom, 69, 74, 76
Time magazine, 24
Tokyo, 42
Topeka, Kansas, 46
Truman, Harry S., 42
Twenty-fourth Infantry Regiment, 42

U

United Nations, 42
United States Solicitor General, 72
United States v. *Nixon*, 9
University of Alabama, 61, 63, 64
University of California, 85
University of Maryland, 14, 16, 17, 18, 19, 20, 21, 61
University of Michigan, 24
University of Missouri, 22, 23, 25, 27
University of Oklahoma, 38, 39, 40, 61
University of Tennessee, 24
University of Texas, 20, 21, 38, 39, 41, 61

V

Vietnam, 88, 93
Vietnam War, 71
Vinson, Fred M., 47, 54
Virginia, 24, 56

W

Wallace, George, 63, 64, 66, 68, 69
Warren, Earl, 54, 56, 58, 72, 95, 96
Washington, D.C., 10, 16, 18, 27, 50
Washington Post, 88
Weddington, Sarah, 78
Wethers, Frank, 27
White, Byron, 79, 83, 98
Wilkins, Roger, 8
Wilkins, Roy, 20
Williams, Karen Hastie, 8
Wilson, Paul, 50, 52
Wisconsin, 69
World War II, 37, 38, 41
writ of madamus, 18

Y

Yechon, 42